The Mystical

Initiations

of Intention

The Path to Self-Mastery, vol 6

The Mystical

Initiations

of Intention

KIM MICHAELS

Copyright © 2016 Kim Michaels. All rights reserved. No part of this book may be used, reproduced, translated, electronically stored or transmitted by any means except by written permission from the publisher. A reviewer may quote brief passages in a review.

MORE TO LIFE PUBLISHING

www.morepublish.com

For foreign and translation rights,

contact info@ morepublish.com

ISBN: 978-87-93297-16-6

The information and insights in this book should not be considered as a form of therapy, advice, direction, diagnosis, and/or treatment of any kind. This information is not a substitute for medical, psychological, or other professional advice, counseling and care. All matters pertaining to your individual health should be supervised by a physician or appropriate health-care practitioner. No guarantee is made by the author or the publisher that the practices described in this book will yield successful results for anyone at any time. They are presented for informational purposes only, as the practice and proof rests with the individual.

For more information: *www.ascendedmasterlight.com and www.transcendencetoolbox.com*

# CONTENTS

Introduction 9

1 | Introducing the Fourth Ray 11

2 | Introducing Serapis Bey 15

3 | The Flame of Acceleration 19

4 | Purity and the Power of Intention 29

5 | Invoking the Power of Intention 49

6 | Pure Intentions for Seeking Wisdom 67

7 | Invoking Wise Intentions 85

8 | From Fear-Based to Love-Based Intentions 103

9 | Invoking Love-Based Intentions 121

10 | Developing Self-Sufficient Intentions 141

11 | Invoking Self-Sufficient Intentions 163

12 | Seeing Opportunities for Self-Transcendence 183

13 | Invoking Pure Vision 205

14 | Finding Peace in Giving Service 225

15 | Invoking Peace in Service 243

16 | Freeing Your Inner Creativity 263

17 | Invoking Freedom to Create 287

4.01 Decree to Astrea and Purity 307

4.02 Decree to Gabriel and Hope 311

4.03 Decree to Serapis Bey 315

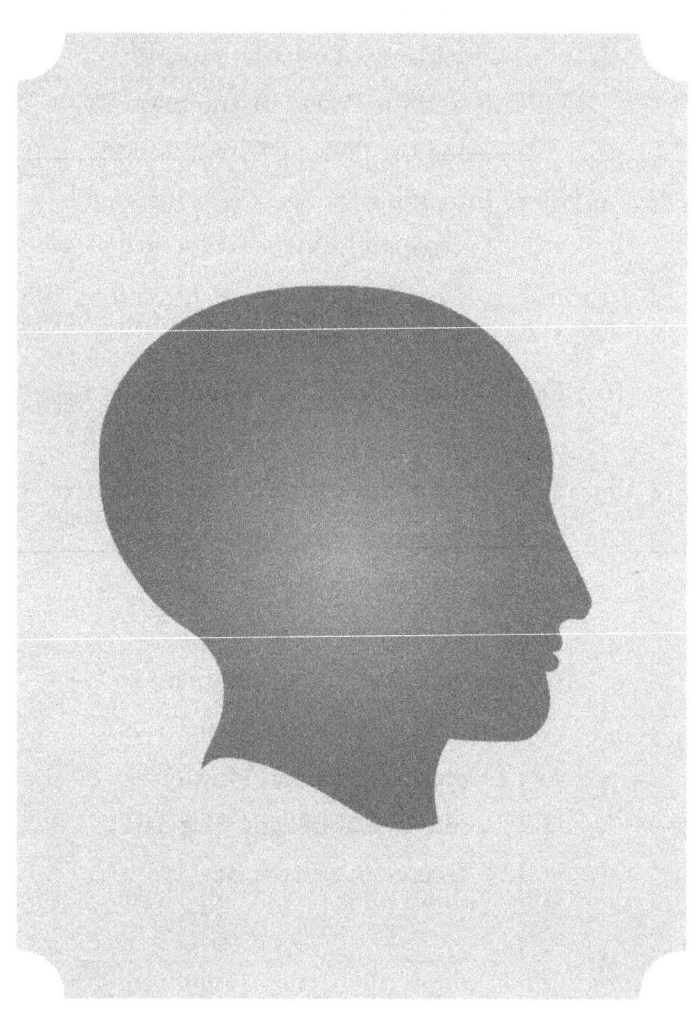

# INTRODUCTION

This book is part of the series *The Path to Self-Mastery*. The purpose of the series is to give you a complete course for knowing and passing the mystical initiations of the seven spiritual rays. The books in the series form a progression, and it is recommended that you start by working through the books to the First Ray of God Power, the Second Ray of God Wisdom and the Third Ray of God Love before progressing to this book.

The purpose of this book is to teach you about the characteristics of the Fourth Ray, which will show you how to purify and accelerate your intentions. If you are new to ascended master teachings, you will benefit greatly from reading the first book in the series, *The Power of Self,* because it gives a general introduction to the spiritual path as it is taught by the ascended masters. This will give you a good foundation for taking greater advantage of the teachings in this book.

This book is designed as a workbook in order to help you better integrate and apply the teachings. You will get the best results if you give the invocation that corresponds to the chapter you are studying. It is recommended that you give a specific invocation once a day for nine days and then study part of the corresponding dictation before or after giving the invocation. Each evening, make calls to be taken to Serapis Bey's retreat in the etheric realm over Luxor in Egypt.

You give an invocation by reading it aloud, thereby invoking high-frequency spiritual energy. For more information about invocations and how to give them, please see the website: *www.transcendencetoolbox.com*. In order to learn more about the ascended masters and how they give dictations, see the website *www.ascendedmasterlight.com*. If you are not familiar with the concepts of the fall and of fallen beings, please read *Cosmology of Evil*. That books gives a profound yet easily understood explanation of why there are some beings who have no respect for the free will (or lives) of human beings. It explains why they are willing to do anything in order to control us or destroy those who will not be controlled.

# 1 | INTRODUCING THE FOURTH RAY

**Color of the Fourth Ray**: Brilliant white
**Corresponding chakra**: Base
**Elohim of the Fourth Ray**: Purity and Astrea
**Archangel and Archeia of the Fourth Ray**: Gabriel and Hope
**Chohan of the Fourth Ray**: Serapis Bey
**Decrees for the Fourth Ray:** 4.01 Decree to Elohim Astrea, 4.02 Decree to Archangel Gabriel, 3.03 Decree to Serapis Bey.

## *Pure qualities of the Fourth Ray*

Traditionally, the Fourth Ray qualities are seen as purity, hope and self-discipline. At a deeper level, the Fourth Ray is the interface between your Spirit and your physical body and the material world. The question asked at the level of the Fourth Ray is whether you will allow the material world to have power over your Spirit so you limit your expression in this world.

The question is whether you believe the current conditions in the material world are real, permanent and unchangeable, or whether you are willing to unleash your creative power in order to accelerate the material world – the Mother element – beyond current conditions.

The Fourth Ray qualities empower you to avoid being trapped in the illusion that the appearances in the material world are real or permanent. You will be able to avoid being trapped in an endless cycle of seeking to fulfill lower, bodily, carnal or human desires. Instead, you will see this world as only a tool for your growth in self-awareness. You will effortlessly avoid activities that do not serve this purpose. This has a deeper layer of understanding, as you will realize it is not a matter of avoiding all human or physical activities—it is a matter of spiritualizing them.

An important illusion to overcome on the spiritual path is the idea that there is a division between the spiritual and the material realm, between spiritual and material activities. Instead, you will be able to remain in oneness, making anything you do a spiritual activity. This will then serve to fulfill the purpose for taking embodiment in the first place, namely to accelerate the vibration of the entire material universe to a higher level where it can become a permanent part of the spiritual realm.

## *Perversions of the Fourth Ray*

Traditionally, the perversions are seen as impurity and chaos. At a deeper level, the perversion is the sense that current conditions are real, are the way they should be or are beyond your power to change. You begin to think this world is separated from the spiritual realm, perhaps even that it belongs to the devil and that you should leave it alone, not seeking to change it. You might even believe you have no right to be a spiritual person in this world or that you have no right to express your spiritual powers in this world. Instead, you think you should accept current conditions and adapt to them.

As the ultimate perversion, you might believe that you are an entirely material being, a product of the material universe—that you have come from dust and that to dust you shall return. In this state of mind, there is no hope of acceleration to a higher state. Given that life itself is acceleration into More, this is a state of mind that Jesus called "death," meaning spiritual death.

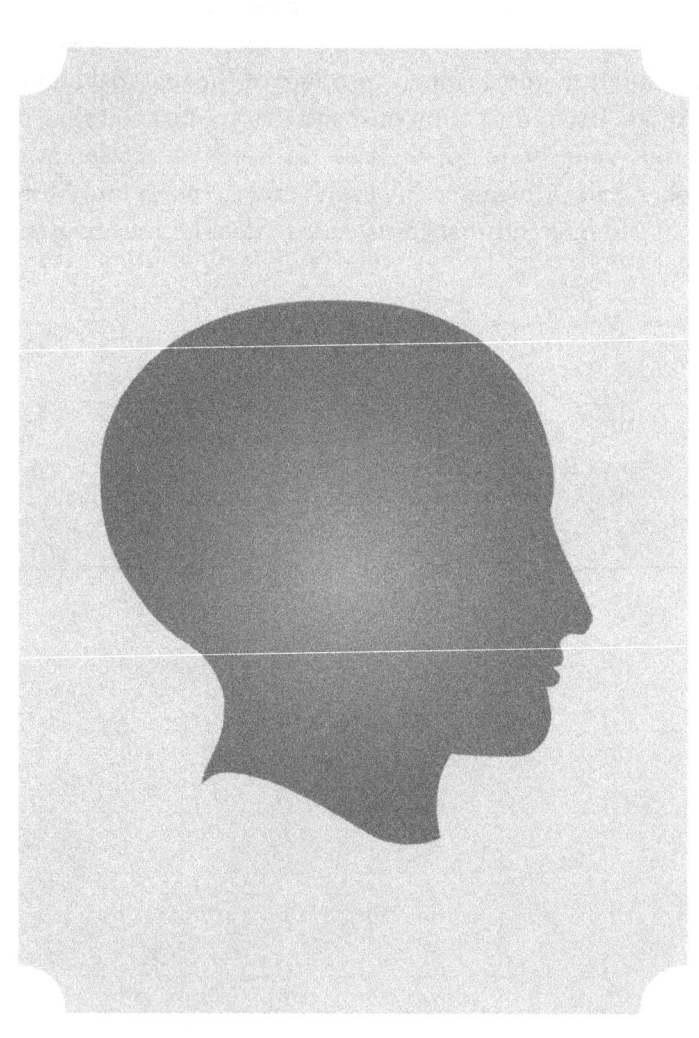

# 2 | INTRODUCING SERAPIS BEY

When you first arrive at Serapis Bey's retreat, located in the etheric realm over Luxor, Egypt, you are put into a group with other lifestreams that are carefully selected so they have the greatest potential for clashing with each other. They have different personalities, karma, backgrounds and different psychological issues. The purpose of this exercise is to quickly expose whether lifestreams are ready for direct contact with Serapis or whether they need more time to prepare for this decisive step on their path.

The temptation is, of course, to engage in various struggles with other lifestreams or engaging in the game of seeking to change others instead of oneself. Those who learned their lessons well under Paul the Venetian, will have learned to love beauty, balance and harmony above the many subtle games of the ego. They will remain focused on changing themselves, and it is precisely this quality for which Serapis is looking. Those who engage in squabbles with others, will have to remain in their groups until they do decide that changing oneself is more important than changing others. They begin to seek harmony and balance even when others seek the opposite.

There are those who say Serapis is a strict disciplinarian, but this is actually not the highest viewpoint, for whom would Serapis be disciplining? Those who still have not left behind the need to struggle, will not even see Serapis so they never experience his discipline. In fact, they discipline each other until some learn to discipline themselves and can move on. Those who do come into direct contact with Serapis have learned to discipline themselves, meaning Serapis has no need to discipline them. He simply provides them with the frame of reference that they need, namely the electrifying purity of the Fourth Ray.

Serapis has an incredible momentum on the ascension flame, which can also be described as the Flame of Acceleration. This white light is not strong in a physical sense where one would think it would shine more brightly. Instead, it is strong in the sense that it accelerates anything that touches it. Only those who are ready for a very strong acceleration of their sense of self can even bear to be in the Presence of Serapis Bey. Given that Serapis has no desire to overload the students, one has to have built a great desire for self-transcendence and an uncompromising willingness to leave behind anything that cannot be accelerated. In the Presence of Serapis, anything that is not capable of being accelerated into the frequencies of the etheric octave will come to light—not all at once but as the student is ready to accelerate beyond it.

Those who are not yet ready for the direct contact, will receive gradual initiations from the capable teachers at the retreat. When ready, they will be allowed to attend special services in the central hall where Serapis demonstrates the invocation of spiritual light, specifically the Flame of Acceleration. They will also be allowed to witness the actual ascension of lifestreams who are ready for this final initiation of earth. Seeing another lifestream be accelerated and rise into the etheric octave is truly one of the greatest forms of inspiration one can receive on the spiritual path. Only those who have some momentum on self-acceleration can actually endure this experience, as for others it can seem like the goal is far beyond their reach, which can become a source of discouragement.

While discouragement has been said to be the sharpest tool in the devil's toolbox, it is a vibration that has little chance of remaining in the retreat at Luxor. A student who will not let go of it cannot remain there, but must go back to one of the retreats of the first three rays. Once you do lock in to the Flame of Acceleration that permeates Serapis Bey's retreat, you will know that there is no condition on earth that cannot be accelerated. You will understand that Serapis is not making an idle promise when he says that you can transcend anything that you are willing to surrender.

Even though a student can receive great acceleration and inspiration by attending Serapis' retreat, it is not possible to ascend from there during one's first attendance. It is indeed necessary to move on to the three remaining rays that form the upper figure in the figure-eight of the spiritual path. You cannot rise to these rays until you have passed through the eye of the needle, the nexus of the Fourth Ray and the accelerating Presence of Serapis.

Perhaps the initiation that requires the greatest courage is to spend some time alone in a room that resembles the King's chamber in the Great Pyramid. You will have to lie in the sarcophagus and experience the etheric parallel to total sensory deprivation. Only when you can endure this initiation in complete harmony and balance, will you be ready for the final step, which is that you meet alone with Serapis in the complete isolation of a stone chamber. Only when you can endure his

Presence, will he send you on with a smile that signals infinite courage and the love that is colored by the white light of the Fourth Ray.

Precisely what it takes to pass the initiation of being alone with Serapis obviously cannot be revealed, as that would take away the uniqueness of the initiation. Furthermore, there is no point in describing what it takes, as the initiation is unique for each person. Only *you* can pass your personal initiation, and what you take with you to the initiation will indeed be sufficient to passing—if you make wise use of it.

# 3 | THE FLAME OF ACCELERATION

Serapis Bey I am, and in the decree I have released, there are a couple of lines that I wish to draw to your attention. They say: "Serapis Bey, your life a poem, that calls me to my starry home." My beloved, ponder this statement, ponder what is implied here, ponder the feelings that it might arouse in you. Then consider, when you look back at world history, that from the earliest civilizations and beyond, people have looked up into the heavens and longed for something, longed for being somewhere else, somewhere out there among the stars, somewhere away from where they are right now here on earth, in these limited physical bodies, in these limited situations that human beings have collectively created.

When people face the return of their karma or the limitations of the matter realm, they often look up into the stars and cry out for freedom. I will not deny, of course, that some of you who will be hearing or reading this teaching, will have come to earth from other planetary systems in other galaxies. Therefore, you might even look up and have some inner memory of a starry home.

Nevertheless, I put these lines in my decree to help you get in contact with the inner longing so that you might come to a higher discernment that there is a false longing and a true longing. The true longing is indeed for oneness with your I AM Presence. Your true starry home is your I AM Presence, not somewhere in the material realm in this physical universe, not some other star system, not some other planet somewhere where life is supposedly better than on earth. I am, of course, not denying that there are planets where life is indeed much better than it is on earth because the planetary collective consciousness has been raised to a higher level.

## Accelerate your sense of self

Nevertheless, my point is this: As long as you long for some better place in the physical realm, you cannot transcend the physical realm, you cannot ascend. Not only that, you cannot truly accelerate into a higher state. You cannot accelerate beyond the state you have when you have passed the initiations of the first three rays and therefore come to the retreat of Serapis Bey, saying: "Serapis, take me further. I have heard that you are the one who can take me further."

I look you squarely in the eye and I say: "Nay, you have heard wrong. I, Serapis Bey, cannot take you further. You are the only one who can take yourself further by accelerating your sense of self. I may play some role in inspiring you to come to the point where you are willing to go through this acceleration,

## 3 | The Flame of Acceleration

but I can do nothing for you. You must be the doer, without being the doer with the outer mind. You must crack the enigma of what it means to accelerate, to truly accelerate, but not in the ego's way; in the way of the Christ."

You must ponder the longings that spring from the ego, the longing for some other place where things are better, which is really a longing away from where you are. You cannot accelerate as long as you long to get away, for acceleration does not mean that you take what is and accelerate it. Acceleration means that you transcend what is by letting go of it, by surrendering it. The key to acceleration is to first surrender that to which you are attached.

You see, my beloved, it is very simple. You may get the idea that what is holding you back on the spiritual path are certain energies that have been absorbed into your auric field. This is not untrue. There *are* energies that are holding you back. You might think that you ascend or rise higher by accelerating these energies. Indeed, you must accelerate the energies, for until you have purified the energies, they will be a dead weight that will hold you back.

Even if you accelerated all of the energies in your auric field, you would not automatically ascend. What must you do then? You must accelerate your sense of self! Here is the difference: Your sense of self is not made of energy, therefore it is not a matter of taking a lower vibration and accelerating that vibration gradually until you reach a higher vibration by crossing the threshold between love and fear. The acceleration of self does not work that way. The acceleration of self is not by accelerating your sense of self from the level it is at to a higher level.

## The quantum leap by letting the old self die

Once you have accepted a sense of self based on the duality consciousness, based on the sense of separation, that ego-based self cannot be accelerated. It can only be allowed to die whereby your sense of self takes a quantum leap. Do you understand, my beloved? Probably you do not, for you have not contemplated this thoroughly. Then, perhaps study a little bit about popular science and see what it actually meant – what a radical departure from previous worldviews it was – when Max Planck discovered that light is not emitted in a continuous stream but in discrete units, which he called "quanta."

You either are the limited self or you are a higher self. There is no gradual path from one to the other. It is not a matter of accelerating the self you have right now. It is a matter of taking the quantum leap by letting the old self die. You are letting go of that life in order to follow Christ and accept the higher sense of self. You attain it by accelerating your self, accelerating what we have called the Conscious You, into a higher state whereby you take on a more Christ-like appearance and likeness.

This is the key that I can teach you in my retreat, if you are willing. So many students come to my retreat without that willingness, and it can take students a very long time to develop that willingness to let the old die. They come to my retreat thinking that they can somehow fool me into helping them accelerate their ego–based self. It is amazing how long students can hold on to this belief; it is amazing how the serpent of the ego will squirm and wiggle around, trying to hide itself from my penetrating eyes, my purifying eyes, and think that it can hide.

It is amazing how long it can take before a student finally one day looks at me, looks me straight in the eyes and accepts:

"I can hide nothing from Serapis so I must either stop trying or I must leave his retreat. For what place do I have here, if I am seeking to hide my ego, if I am seeking to do the impossible? I am only fooling myself. I will never fool Serapis."

## Initiations at the Retreat of Serapis Bey

If they do not walk out of here at that moment, as some indeed do, they will look at my penetrating eyes and they will see my love. When they feel that love, then they can let the old die. They know that I will carry them in my arms until they have accepted that new sense of self. *That* is what I can do for you in my retreat. I can give you the sense that there will be something after the death of the limited self. I cannot carry you there. You must indeed let go and let the old die.

We do, of course, have various processes at my retreat that are aimed at helping people overcome this interim stage where they are still seeking to hide the ego. One I have already talked about several times before, and that is to put people into groups with other lifestreams with which they have various clashes. They have to work it out until they decide that acceleration is more important than playing these ego-based games. We do have another tool that I wish to bring to your attention.

It is something you may indeed contemplate, as you contemplate the journey beyond the Third Ray into the realm of the Fourth Ray of acceleration and purity. There is a room at my retreat; if you would describe it physically, you would say that it is a room with a very intricate geometry. It is not exactly spherical, for the walls are made up of smaller facets in various geometrical shapes. These facets are covered with a material that in an earthly sense would be like a mirror, but it is not a physical mirror that reflects visible light. It is a material that reflects any kind of energy that vibrates in the emotional, mental and etheric realm.

For those who are ready – for those who have reached a certain level, and certainly for those who have gone beyond the petty squabbles with others – they have the opportunity to enter this room where they will be, so to speak, suspended by an intricate harness that keeps them suspended in the center of the room without them directly touching any of the walls. The purpose for this is to make sure that they are not touching any of the reflecting surfaces. When the door is closed and a certain switch is turned on, what will happen is that the material on the surfaces will now begin to reflect back to you from all directions anything you are sending out with the subconscious and conscious mind.

Normally, as you are in physical embodiment on earth, you are, of course, constantly projecting out various mental images, various energies with your subconscious mind, with your emotional, mental and identity mind. You do not immediately feel a return of this because as the energy is projected out, it in most cases takes a while before it comes back, as it cycles through the material universe and through the three other realms of the material spectrum.

We have given you the concept of karma in its most primitive form of a linear concept. Certainly, we have also given you, by Master MORE, a more sophisticated understanding of karma. Much of what you encounter today as limitations, as a burden of energy, is karma from a past life. Therefore, you do not see any direct connection between cause and effect.

You are only seeing what came back, and you are not seeing what you sent out because of the time delay. This is both a grace and an opportunity, but it, of course, has the effect that you do not directly see what you sent out to cause the karmic return. When you go into the reflection room at my retreat, the time delay is removed. You are now instantly feeling a return of what you are sending out. Only, what you are feeling is a return that cannot be hidden by anything in your own being.

## The reflection room

You will feel with your conscious mind what you are sending out with the subconscious mind. We will allow students at a certain level the opportunity to enter this room. For many students at the beginning phases of this initiation, we will close the door, turn on the switch and turn it off again after exactly seven seconds. Seven seconds, one for each of the seven rays. For many students this is all they can bear and almost more than they can bear. In those seven seconds, they feel such an intensity of what they are constantly projecting out with their subconscious minds that they can barely stand it. Were we to allow them to remain there any longer, the experience would be so shattering that it might take them a long time to recover. This is, of course, not our intention whatsoever.

You understand that a student can only enter this reflection room when he or she has asked for it and understands fully what is happening. It is, indeed, an extremely valuable experience, for suddenly you experience consciously what you are sending out subconsciously—but which you are not experiencing consciously. You know how much your subconscious mind is actually projecting out beyond your conscious awareness and consent. You now have the opportunity to work on this, and, of course, you receive the loving guidance of both myself and other assistants in my retreat. No one is allowed to have this experience without receiving the proper guidance for how to process and use it. I give you this teaching so that you might understand the possibility of you knowing consciously what you are sending out subconsciously. It is indeed a great opportunity, and I can tell you that there is no greater joy than when a student has gone through the process in my retreat of entering the reflection room, receiving help to overcome its subconscious momentums and has gradually, often over a long time, purified itself from all the subconscious momentums. It can now enter the reflection room without being so burdened by the subconscious momentums that it cannot realize that it is also sending out higher vibrations, vibrations that vibrate beyond the threshold of love. When a student is no longer so shocked by its lower momentums that it begins to tune in to the higher, well, then the student has passed an important threshold.

## *Walking the earth as the SUN of God*

Now it begins to see, indeed, how much of a positive impact one being can have by radiating positive energy on earth. As a student progresses, purifies its being even more, it can come to that point where it knows it is sending out only love-based vibrations, and this is, indeed, a great turning point. Now a student, before it has actually ascended, can walk the earth as the sun – S-U-N – of God, radiating only the higher vibrations. This is precisely why I give you this teaching.

You can apply, with your conscious mind, to go through this process, if you feel you are ready. I offer you the opportunity that as you give the invocations in this book, you can ask me with a simple statement before you go to bed at night, that you will be taken to my retreat and that you will be allowed to have some sense, as you can bear it with your conscious mind, of both what you are sending out of lower vibrations and of higher vibrations so that you may have the opportunity

## 3 | The Flame of Acceleration

to correct yourself. This, my beloved, is a great opportunity for anyone willing to go through this. It may not be easy, it may not be pleasant. Then again, it may also be very rewarding and pleasant for you to realize how much positive momentum you actually have. Naturally, we do not show you only the lower momentums but the higher as well. I can assure you that if you are willing to work through this book, then you will have more positive than not-so-positive momentums. Otherwise, you simply could not have come to this point, you could not have followed the other books for the first three rays, as I assume you have done before you consider using this book to the Fourth Ray.

Do not think that your decrees or invocations are in vain. When you enter the reflection room and see how much positive energy you are sending out, you begin to realize the truth that many do not normally consider. Whereas you do not know the lower momentums of what you are projecting out, you do not normally know the higher momentums either until you receive some positive karmic return of something from a past life. If you will tune in, I will give you some impression of the positive momentums that you are sending out, the positive energies that you are radiating to this planet. This can be a great encouragement for your future work for the ascended masters and your future growth towards that ultimate goal: the ascension.

The Fourth Ray must be either an acceleration point or a deceleration point. It is difficult to stand still for long in the energies of the Fourth Ray. Be not concerned about those who decelerate, even people around you or in your personal sphere of influence. There are many who must decelerate and act out to the extreme whatever momentums they have that are still subconscious, for they have not recognized them. Be not concerned about this, be concerned only about your own acceleration and then possibly inspiring others to accelerate as well when they see that you are not burdened by what burdens them.

My purpose is to encourage you to accelerate your being, and therefore I welcome those to the retreat of Serapis Bey who are willing to be accelerated beyond any impurities in their being. For *that* Flame of Acceleration, I AM.

# 4 | PURITY AND THE POWER OF INTENTION

I AM the ascended master Serapis Bey. I am the Chohan of the Fourth Ray. As you know, it has often been called the ray of purity but I have also called it the ray of acceleration. It is, of course, a combination of both, for how do you purify something unless you accelerate it?

What I want to point out in this discourse is exactly what this course is about and what the goal is on the first level of initiation at my retreat. We have called this course: A Course in Self-Mastery. Ponder the word "self-mastery." You are mastering the Self, you are not mastering the world or other people. You are mastering the Self. Through mastery of the Self you may indeed be able to influence your environment, your surroundings, your personal situation, but you will not be able to influence other people in the sense that you force them to comply with your desires.

## The purpose of mind over matter

We have also said that the purpose of this course is to raise you from the 48th to the 96th level of consciousness. We have said that as you approach the 96th level, you will achieve the mastery of mind over matter. This I want to discourse on, for it is often something that is misunderstood by spiritual students of all kinds, including ascended master students.

You can find books in the world that are aimed at giving people the power of precipitation, precipitating whatever they want, often riches or gold, for example. Our course is not directed at helping you precipitate riches or other things you want in the sense that you bring it forth "out of the blue" so to speak.

The mastery of mind over matter that we aim to give you is not a matter of performing party tricks that can impress other people or performing actions that can enrich yourself. We are not seeking to teach you some kind of black magic whereby you can control matter or the external world while still having so much ego that you are doing it from a self-centered perspective.

This mastery of mind over matter is, of course, something that we desire to see you develop, but it must be developed in total synchronicity with the mastery of self. What you too often see in the world is that there are people who desire to have some kind of mastery over matter whereby they, for example, can manifest certain things, but they are not willing to follow the course of attaining mastery over self. This, of course, is not what we of the ascended masters teach to our real students.

# 4 | Purity and the Power of Intention

## *Self-mastery is not a mechanical skill*

I want to point something out to you that many ascended master students have not understood. Self-mastery is not a task you can learn in the same way as you learn, for example, to drive a car. Many of the skills that are required in order to do well in the world have a somewhat mechanical nature. They can be mastered to a certain degree by almost anyone who is willing to apply themselves to practicing the skill. There may be some that will never learn to drive a car beyond the ordinary level, but many can learn to drive a car at a fairly high level, even a professional level, if they apply enough time and practice.

There are many, many spiritual students throughout the ages who have approached self-mastery the same way. They think it is a mechanical path that you can follow. If you take all of the steps outlined, then you will automatically attain the mastery promised. You will see that there are many organizations or even teachers who claim that they can take you on a course of initiation, a path of initiation, and this will give you some special abilities.

This is not how the ascended masters teach. We are not concerned about you having specific abilities, whether it be clairvoyance or the ability to manifest things. This is not our concern at all. Our concern is the raising of your consciousness, which is achieved through self-mastery. Or you may say that self-mastery is achieved through the raising of your consciousness, whatever you prefer.

The raising of consciousness is not a mechanical path. Going back into the mists of history, there have always been certain schools, organizations or gurus who have claimed that they can take their students on a mechanical path. You know, for example that the Freemasons have 33 levels of initiation, and when you go through these steps of initiation, you get a certain title. Many other schools and gurus are the same way. If you go through the outer initiations and if you do not fail miserably, then you will automatically get a title.

You see, of course, the same in the educational institutions of the world. If you study a certain topic long enough and if you fulfill certain outer requirements, you will get a degree. You now have a diploma saying that you are supposedly an expert in this or that topic. Does having a diploma saying you are a psychologist necessarily mean that you have an intuitive feel for what psychology is all about, including your own psychology and how it works? Well, as many have demonstrated, it does not, and it is the same for the path of initiation under the ascended masters.

## The false path of the fallen beings

There is always a danger in giving a set of books that describe the initiations you go through at the seven retreats of the Chohans when you are following the path to self-mastery. Anyone can buy the book and read the lessons and perform the invocations and thereby take the outer steps.

There is, of course, a reason why we start at the First Ray and build up through there. We of the Chohans coordinate our efforts so that we have a coordinated plan. It is clearly only valid for a student to start at the First Ray, go through the Second, then the Third and then finally the Fourth Ray that I represent. When you have a book that contains the teachings and initiations, it is quite possible that someone can buy this book without having gone through the other three. It will, when all books are completed, be possible that someone can buy the set, go through from the first one to the seventh, read all the lessons, perform all the invocations and then they will think they have completed the course. That is not the way it works on the true path of initiation.

The fallen beings, which we have sometimes called the false hierarchy, have indeed attempted to create a mechanical path of initiation. Their dream is that if you go through certain outer steps and fulfill certain outer requirements, then you will automatically acquire a certain title or even certain abilities.

It is possible, at least for some people, to attain a certain mastery over matter without having purified the self and thereby attained self-mastery. This, of course, is the dream of the fallen beings. They do not want to purify the self, they do not want to attain true self-mastery. In fact, they do not want to attain *self*-mastery, they want to attain the mastery of being able to control other people or even physical matter.

## Self-mastery is not control of the self

You see, my beloved, there are people who think that self-mastery means you can control the self. There are even ascended master students who have followed ascended master teachings for decades and who still believe that I, Serapis Bey, am the primary disciplinarian. They think that I serve you up a set of disciplinary rules. If you follow my rules and endure my discipline, then they think they will be able to control the self. Many, many students have attempted to control the self.

Why am I talking about this in the first lesson? It is because the first lesson is, of course, the combination of the First Ray of Power and the Fourth Ray of Purity. What is control? It is one of the primary perversions of the First Ray of Power, as my beloved colleague, Master MORE, explained in his book. We are not aiming this course at helping you control the self by forcing your body and your outer mind to live up to a set of outer rules and standards. Let me make one thing perfectly clear to you, as clear as it can be done, given the state of consciousness that people are at when they are likely to read this book.

## You cannot hide anything from Serapis

There is a line in my decree: "Serapis Bey what power lies, behind your purifying eyes." Well, my eyes are purifying because they are also penetrating. They see through all impurities and the smokescreens that have been created by impurities. What do impurities do? When water is impure, it is often unclear so you cannot see through it.

So often those who are still trapped in a lower state of consciousness have such impurities in their minds that you cannot clearly see their intentions. When I say "you," I mean people in general. Many students have come having seemingly benign intentions in their conscious minds but having not so benign intentions in their subconscious minds. Only, they are not able to see them because of the impurities that obscure the subconscious mind.

My eyes are purifying because they penetrate all of these smokescreens. You may say: "Well, are you then not violating people's privacy?" Well, my beloved, I do not go around in the world and look at every human being with my penetrating eyes. When you take this book, you should have in your conscious mind an intention to submit yourself to the initiations under me as the Chohan of the Fourth Ray. How do you submit yourself to my initiations, if you are not willing to have me look at you?

I am not in any way trying to force you. I am only trying to help you see that it makes no sense to have the intention in your mind that you want to follow the initiations of the Fourth Ray under Serapis Bey, but at the same time there is something you want to hide from me.

You see my beloved, I am not the kind of disciplinarian that many people imagine based on their worldly experiences. I am not a drill sergeant in the army who enjoys finding fault with you and who will point it out mercilessly in front of a crowd if given the opportunity. I am not here to scold you. I am not here to shame you. I am not here to put you down in any way. I am not even the strict disciplinarian that many people think I am. I am the master of the Fourth Ray of Purity. You cannot purify something if you will not see the impurity. It cannot be done, my beloved. Why do so many people think it can be done? Because they have been affected by the fallen consciousness.

One of the essential elements of the fallen consciousness is, of course, that the fallen beings do not want to face God. They do not want to face the spiritual teacher from the ascended realm. It is not difficult to get into the ascended realm; you only need to purify your consciousness of all of the things that magnetize you to the material realm, to the unascended sphere. The fallen beings are not willing to do this, and many of them do not even understand the need to do this. They still think that they can force their way into heaven by hiding something from the ascended masters.

There are many students who come to my retreat and they still think they can pass the seven levels of initiation at my retreat while hiding their true intentions from me. My beloved, this makes no sense. Can you not see this? There is no cheating on the path of initiation under the ascended masters. We have said that the Fourth Ray forms the nexus of the figure-eight of the flow between the initiations of the first three rays and those of the last three. It is, so to speak, "the eye of the needle." As you know from the Bible, it is easier for a camel to pass through the eye of the needle than it is for a rich man to enter heaven. What is a rich man? It is one who thinks he owns something in this world and wants to take it with him through that eye of the needle. Those who come and think they own something – and they want to bring it with them into the ascended state, they want to bring it into my retreat and they want to bring it through my retreat to the higher rays – they are like the rich man.

What is the purpose of purification? Is it not to let go of things that hold you back. How can you let go of something unless you look at it? There is no *unconscious* surrender, there is no unconscious letting go; it can only be *conscious*. It makes no sense whatsoever to think that you can pass the initiations in my retreat and still hide something from me. My beloved, what makes even less sense is to think you can pass the initiations in my retreat while still hiding something from yourself.

## Self-mastery and hiding things from yourself

The course is a course in *self*-mastery. How can you master the self if there are aspects of the self – pockets of the self – that you are not willing to look at? This is impossible. Many people think that self-mastery means that you are controlling the self by suppressing the elements of the self that are not acceptable according to an outer standard. This is not how it works at my retreat. There is no outer standard. I am not a disciplinarian that imposes an outer standard on you and demands that you live up to it. I impose no standard on you when you come to my retreat. Does that mean there is no standard imposed upon you? Well, in a sense we could say that there *is* a standard, but the standard is defined by *you!* It is defined by the impurities that you carry with you when you walk through the gate.

You see, my beloved, there is a gate that gives you entry to my retreat. You can at any time decide that you have had enough of the initiations in my retreat and you can leave my retreat through the same gate that you entered. The purpose of passing the seven levels of initiation is that you get to the other gate in my retreat, the one that leads up to the next level of initiation under the next Chohan.

You see, my beloved, there is no way to get to *that* retreat and still carry with you the impurities that you took with you into *my* retreat. You cannot exit my retreat through the higher door while carrying the stuff with you that you took in through the entry door. The impurities must be transformed, the energy must be transformed.

Behind the energy is a belief you have about yourself and the world. This belief was entered into, accepted into your mind, by a decision you made. Unless you uncover that decision, see the limitations behind it and consciously replace it with a higher decision, you are not free of the impurity. If you are not free of the impurity, how can you rise to the next level of initiation? There is an entry door, there is an exit door but there are doors in between. For each level you go up, there is a door you must pass through. You cannot pass through the second door while carrying the impurities you are supposed to let go of at the first level of initiation.

There is no cheating here, my beloved. There is no hiding anything. You cannot hide anything from me. You can enter my retreat at the first level and still hide something from yourself—*that* is allowed. You will not get beyond the first level while still hiding something from yourself. It is not possible, my beloved. I know that your ego will come up with all kinds of reasons why it must be possible but it *is not* possible. I am the Chohan and I have seen millions of students come to my retreat, many of them leaving again because they would not look at what they needed to look at in order to rise to the next level of initiation. I have no condemnation for this, but I cannot help you if you are not willing to look at yourself.

## Group conflicts

You may have heard or read that when people first come to my retreat, they are put in groups with other souls with whom they have clashing personality, astrology, karma and other characteristics. It has been said that you will not go further until you have realized that harmony is more important than all of these conflicts. Well, we can look at this initiation in other ways.

When people are first put together in these groups, where they have the greatest opportunity to clash with each other, the real initiation is to come to a point where you pass the major hurdle on the spiritual path. I know you can say that for each level of consciousness there is a major hurdle. There is a big hurdle from the 48th to the 49th level of consciousness. But on the spiritual path – the path of self-mastery – the major hurdle is to come to a point where you are no longer seeking to change other people or the material world.

On the first three levels of initiation there are many students that are taking these initiations because they have a hidden, or maybe not-so-hidden, intention of being able to gain the power to control other people and their own environment. They want to control their situation so that they can get the exact conditions that they think they need in order to attain whatever they want to attain, perhaps inner harmony, perhaps peace of mind, perhaps certain outer conditions and experiences.

You would be surprised at how many students come to my retreat while still having the desire to exercise power for the purpose of control, the desire to attain power in order to be able to control their situation. What is it that people are really trying to do when they seek to control other people or their environment? Well, they are seeking to produce a state of mind. Everything that happens in the material realm is experienced through your mind. It is your mind, the contents of your mind, the structures, the matrices in your mind, that will determine how you experience a certain outer situation. As we have explained many times, two people can have a very different inner experience based on the same outer situation. These people are attempting to change their inner situation by exercising control of their outer situation.

First of all, this cannot be done beyond a certain level. It can be done to some degree, as some people in the world have demonstrated. You can see some very rich and powerful people who have attained some degree of control over their environment. Many of these have been high-ranking fallen beings who have gained this control through their practice for a very, very long time span, often spanning their fall through several spheres.

Surely, such people, by practicing for such a long period of time, can gain some mastery over the matter realm and some ability to control other people. Is this really what you are striving for as an ascended master student? If you have not already gained this mastery, do you think you can gain it in the rest of this lifetime? If you cannot, then you will have to re-embody again for eons of time until you attain this mastery, or rather control over matter. Is this really what you want?

## Purifying your intention

You see, my beloved, the first level of initiation at my retreat is the combination of power and purity, but what do you need in order to exercise power? You need an intention, you need a motive. The first level of my retreat is all about helping you purify your intention, your motives.

Why do I put people together in groups with whom they have the biggest chance of clashing? Because it is one of the most effective ways of bringing out the hidden motives, the hidden intentions. You see so many times where these students are attempting to control each other. What often happens in a group is that two people emerge as the strongest, those who have the strongest desire to be in control. These two people will, as the popular saying goes, "lock horns" and seek to dominate each other and the group. Well, surely these are not the two who are ready to go to the next level at my retreat, are they? They may think they are because they are powerful, they think, but what good is power if you do not have the intention?

Do you see that in the world, the fallen beings have done everything they could possibly do to attain physical power without having the purity of intention? Adolph Hitler had physical power to round up six million people and put them in concentration camps and kill most of them. Joseph Stalin had physical power to round up even more millions of people and put them in concentrations camps and execute them. The great Chairman Mao had even greater power than Stalin. They had physical power but was their intention pure? Certainly not if it involves killing other human beings. I assume you will agree with this.

Physical power has nothing to do with the purity of intention. Those who have the purity of intention will be extremely reluctant to exercise or demonstrate physical power. We have a considerable amount of students who come to my retreat having studied and practiced ascended master teachings for a while. They often have a dream that they will attain some kind of special power; some powers of the Spirit, even the Gifts of the Holy Spirit that are talked about by various groups. Many times these students have this desire because they think, in their conscious minds, that if they gain these abilities, they could use them to demonstrate and prove to other people that the spiritual path works. They think they could convert millions of people to follow an ascended master teaching.

Why is it that we of the ascended masters do not just appear in the sky or appear among people and prove our existence? Well, it is because we respect the Law of Free Will and we respect the kind of initiations that planet earth is designed to give. What good would it do to attract millions of people to ascended master teachings if they were not yet at the level where they had the purity of intention to learn the things that we teach? We are not out to attract numbers. Why would it interest us? We are not interested in having billions of followers who are not ready to follow the path of initiation that we offer. Therefore, we are not interested in having our students focus their attention on developing special abilities with an impure intention that is not in alignment with our intention. Do you not see this? The first level of initiation at my retreat on the path of self-mastery is all aimed at helping you purify your intentions. First, you must be in a group with other people and you must come to the point where you have demonstrated that you have no intention of changing other people in order to make yourself feel a certain way. You have no intention of dominating or controlling other people; you have no intention of dominating or controlling matter in order to make yourself feel a certain way. Your intention is to master the self, not by *controlling* the self but by *mastering* the self.

## The elements of self-mastery

What is self-mastery? Well, the first element of self-mastery is to purify yourself, your four lower bodies, from all of the impurities that you have picked up during your many incarnations on earth or other planets. It is these impurities that pull you into certain patterns. It may be patterns of actions, patterns of feelings, patterns of thoughts or certain patterns of identity. You are constantly being pulled into these patterns and this, of course, is not self-mastery.

Your first step is to purify your mind of these patterns. It is not a matter of exercising control and suppressing the patterns or replacing them with more powerful patterns. This is not self-*mastery*. It may be self-*control* but that is not what we are looking for in our students. That is what the fallen teachers, the false hierarchy, are looking for in their students, but we are looking for self-mastery. This is attained by looking at all of the impurities in your consciousness and consciously letting them go and deciding on a higher intention.

It may be that at some of the higher levels of consciousness before you ascend, you can attain a certain mastery over matter, like Jesus demonstrated. It may be that you will attain this mastery. It may be that you will even demonstrate it, but it may also be that you will not demonstrate it, as many people have done (or not done) throughout history. Many people have attained a certain mastery over matter without ever demonstrating it for other people because they understood that this is not the highest intent.

The purpose of this course, of taking you from the 48th to the 96th level of consciousness, is *not* to have you perform some impressive feats but to have you attain self-mastery and that means, first of all, purifying your mind of what pulls you into lesser patterns. It also means purifying your motives, your intention, so that you bring yourself into alignment with the intention of the ascended masters.

You see, my beloved, it is not that walking the spiritual path means you put on a straitjacket. I am not here saying that, as you come closer to the 144th level of consciousness, there is nothing you can do because you always have to follow the intent of the hierarchy above you. What I am saying is that, as you get closer and closer to the 144th level, you come more and more into alignment with the hierarchy above you.

## Purification and free will

This does not mean that you do not have free will, but it does mean that you are exercising your free will in a way that is so radically different from what you envision at your present level of consciousness that I cannot actually describe it in words. It would do no good to describe to you, at your present level, what you will attain at levels that are so much higher, for we are not trying to give you an impossible ideal. What I am trying to give you is a sense that on the path of self-mastery, there is a certain period where you do need to surrender all lesser intentions. You do this in practicality by tuning in to the intentions of the Chohan under which you are working—me on the Fourth Ray, Hilarion on the Fifth Ray, and so on.

When you are at a certain retreat, you purify your intention by attuning to the intention of the Chohan of that retreat and bringing yourself into alignment with that intent. That means you will be surrendering your ego-based intentions, and your ego, of course, will experience this as a restriction. It will try to make you believe that this is a restriction of your free will and it is like putting on a straitjacket. In reality, it is like taking off the straitjacket of the ego that you are presently wearing, but I agree that this is difficult to see for a certain period of time. Therefore, I am warning you that there will come a time, and there will come an initiation at the first level of my retreat, where you have to use conscious willpower to bring yourself beyond the intentions of the ego for exercising power.

The ego will come up with all kinds of excuses for why you should exercise power, for example to impress people and attract ascended master students or do some other good things in the world. You need to use your conscious willpower to accelerate yourself beyond it, not by suppressing it but by looking at the intention and then comparing it to the intention that I will demonstrate to you.

You will experience at inner levels, when you go through the first initiation at my retreat, my intention, the intention of those who are working on the Fourth Ray. You will experience the contrast. As I have said, we have no intention of controlling people or violating free will or forcing initiations on people for which they are not ready. You must reach that same level by letting go of all of these fanciful desires of doing wonderful things in the world or of controlling your environment.

## True mastery over matter

It is true that as you approach the 96th level, you will attain a certain mastery of mind over matter, but it will not be in the fanciful way that you can suddenly precipitate something out of thin air. It will actually be that you demonstrate a higher way to live so that you are living in the material world but your life is an expression of your own higher being, your I AM Presence. You are not living a life according to the standards of the world, especially not the standards of the fallen beings. You are living according to a higher vision, a higher intention that is very different from what most people see in the world. This is not a matter of demonstrating some kind of mastery by being more powerful, richer or more beautiful than others. It is a matter of demonstrating that you are following a higher vision that is not dualistic, that is not aimed at raising yourself in comparison to others or even by putting other people down. You are seeking to raise the All, but you are, first of all, seeking to purify and master yourself.

This is the kind of mastery we seek to give you in this course. If you long for another kind of mastery, and if you have so far thought that this course would give you that mastery, then the first level of initiation at my retreat is the time to reconsider. If you cannot let go of these desires, then it is a good time to leave my retreat, to leave this path and go and seek some kind of guru that will promise you this outer mastery through control. I respect your free will. I am not seeking to hold you at my retreat if you are not ready for the initiations I offer. For many students who come to my retreat – often with the best of intentions (they think) but not really the highest of intentions – it can be quite a shock at this first level. It is sort of a sifting period. We "separate the chaff from the wheat," as they say. Not in a sense that *we* go around doing it but that we allow people themselves to more clearly see their intentions.

It is not that I condemn anyone for having an intention of experiencing some kind of mastery through control. As we have said before, the things that are happening on earth can only happen because a certain amount of the people embodied on earth desire a certain type of experience. If you desire to have the experience of being able to control others or control matter – without looking at yourself – then I simply cannot help you. I do not condemn you, but I recommend that you go elsewhere to seek the experience and then come back when you are ready for what I offer.

## Some will want a different path

I am not a disciplinarian according to the worldly definition of it. On the other hand, you cannot fool me, you cannot cheat me, you cannot hide anything from me. If your intention is not in alignment with the purpose of this course of self-mastery, then you cannot walk through the gate that leads from the first level of initiation to the second level of initiation at my retreat. You can stay at the first level for as long as you like. You can stay in groups with other people who also have the same problem of letting go of their intentions.

You can stay there for *almost* as long as you like, or you can exit through the same door through which you entered. That is *your* choice. I am not a disciplinarian. You are the one who is disciplining by projecting an image upon me. Many of the students who leave often leave by projecting an image upon me that I did not live up to their expectations, that I did not do this, that I did not do that.

This only demonstrates that they are not done with the experience of using other people or external circumstances as an excuse for not looking at themselves. If they need me to be that excuse, then I can only let them. If they are in the state of mind where they are projecting an image upon me, and using it as an excuse, there is usually nothing I could say that will help them see what they are doing. Of course, as any true teacher, if I cannot help the student, I will not force that student. What I will do in some cases is intensify the light of purity to a point where those who will not let go of their impure intentions simply cannot stand being there.

We put lifestreams together in groups. In rare cases, a group will not go anywhere. In most cases, the groups will gradually come to a point where people have had enough of the arguing and the fighting. They start asking themselves and each other: "We see that people in the world have been arguing and fighting for thousands of years without getting anywhere, why are we doing the same at this retreat? Is that really why we are here? Did we not come here to listen to what Serapis Bey has to offer? So why are we sitting here arguing with each other?" When they reach that point, they are ready for more direct interaction with me so I can help them pass the initiations of the first level and move on to the second.

In rare cases, a group will not reach this point. They will keep standing in the same place. Now, because they are at my retreat, I do have the right to turn up the light, to increase the intensity. I cannot do this in the world at large, but I can do this for those that have voluntarily entered my retreat. I turn up the light, and this means that the people will now *not* be able to ignore the impurities in their consciousness. They must either look at them and work on them or they must make a greater effort to deny them, to explain them away.

If people continue to do this, there can come a point where I will turn up the light so much that they can no longer remain in the retreat but make up some excuse for why they have to leave. There are also those who come to the point where they see that they want to leave because they want a different kind of experience. This is, of course, fine. With those students I can have a point of saying goodbye, and we can be in accord with each other in the sense that we both realize what is best for the student.

Those who will not admit that they are leaving out of their own choosing, but project some kind of excuse upon me, well, those I cannot have that little parting meeting with. They most often leave in a huff, often without looking back, sometimes even while cursing me as they walk out the door. Those I cannot help until the School of Hard Knocks has given them so many knocks that they are now ready to knock on my door again. At which point I, of course, will receive them, but I will also exercise my right to say, right away: "Have you now learned the lesson you were not willing to learn the first time you were here?"

Therefore, I end this somewhat sombre discourse by saying to all students who consider entering my retreat: "Have you considered what awaits you when you step through that door? Have you considered the purpose of the initiation that you are saying you are willing to embark upon? Are you ready for what I offer? If you are, then I welcome you with open arms and an open heart and *very* open eyes. If you are willing to open your eyes, I am the Chohan who will help you do so."

Serapis Bey I AM.

# 5 | INVOKING THE POWER OF INTENTION

In the name I AM THAT I AM, Jesus Christ, I call to my I AM Presence to flow through the I Will Be Presence that I AM and give this invocation with full power. I call to beloved Elohim Purity and Astrea and Hercules and Amazonia, Archangel Gabriel and Hope and Michael and Faith, Serapis Bey and Master MORE to help me transcend all impure desires and intentions for exercising power. Help me see and surrender all patterns that block my oneness with Serapis Bey and with my I AM Presence, including …

[Make personal calls]

## Part 1

1. Serapis Bey, I consciously surrender all desires for mastering the world or other people, all desires for influencing other people by forcing them to comply with my desires.

Beloved Astrea, your heart is so true,
your Circle and Sword of white and blue,
cut all life free from dramas unwise,
on wings of Purity our planet will rise.

**Beloved Astrea, in God Purity,
accelerate all of my life energy,
raising my mind into true unity
with the Masters of love in Infinity.**

2. Serapis Bey, I consciously surrender all desires for the power of precipitation, the ability to precipitate whatever I want, such as riches or gold, "out of the blue."

Beloved Astrea, from Purity's Ray,
send forth deliverance to all life today,
acceleration to Purity, I AM now free
from all that is less than love's Purity.

**Beloved Astrea, in oneness with you,
your circle and sword of electric blue,
with Purity's Light cutting right through,
raising within me all that is true.**

3. Serapis Bey, I consciously surrender all desires for performing party tricks that can impress other people or performing actions that can enrich myself.

Beloved Astrea, accelerate us all,
as for your deliverance I fervently call,
set all life free from vision impure
beyond fear and doubt, I AM rising for sure.

## 5 | Invoking the Power of Intention

**Beloved Astrea, I AM willing to see,
all of the lies that keep me unfree,
I AM rising beyond every impurity,
with Purity's Light forever in me.**

4. Serapis Bey, I consciously surrender all desires for learning black magic whereby I can control matter or the external world from a self-centered perspective.

Beloved Astrea, accelerate life
beyond all duality's struggle and strife,
consume all division between God and man,
accelerate fulfillment of God's perfect plan.

**Beloved Astrea, I lovingly call,
break down separation's invisible wall,
I surrender all lies causing the fall,
forever affirming the oneness of All.**

5. Serapis Bey, I consciously desire to develop mastery of mind over matter in total synchronicity with the mastery of self. I am willing to follow the course of attaining mastery over self.

O Hercules Blue, you fill every space,
with infinite Power and infinite Grace,
you embody the key to creativity,
the will to transcend into Infinity.

**O Hercules Blue, in oneness with thee,
I open my heart to your reality,
in feeling your flame, so clearly I see,
transcending my self is the true alchemy.**

6. Serapis Bey, I consciously surrender all desires for developing self-mastery through a mechanical path where I take certain outer steps and then automatically attain the mastery promised.

> O Hercules Blue, I lovingly raise,
> my voice in giving God infinite praise,
> I'm grateful for playing my personal part,
> In God's infinitely intricate work of art.
>
> **O Hercules Blue, all life now you heal,**
> **enveloping all in your Blue-flame Seal,**
> **your electric-blue fire within us reveal,**
> **our innermost longing for all that is real.**

7. Serapis Bey, I consciously surrender all desires for discovering a path of initiation that will give me some special abilities, such as clairvoyance or the ability to manifest things.

> O Hercules Blue, I pledge now my life,
> in helping this planet transcend human strife,
> duality's lies are pierced by your light,
> restoring the fullness of my inner sight.
>
> **O Hercules Blue, I'm one with your will,**
> **all space in my being with Blue Flame you fill,**
> **your power allows me to forge on until,**
> **I pierce every veil and climb every hill.**

8. Serapis Bey, I consciously surrender all desires for following the schools, organizations or gurus who claim they can take me on a mechanical path whereby I automatically get a title.

## 5 | Invoking the Power of Intention

O Hercules Blue, your Temple of Light,
revealed to us all through our inner sight,
a beacon that radiates light to the Earth,
bringing about our planet's rebirth.

**O Hercules Blue, all life you defend,
giving us power to always transcend,
in you the expansion of self has no end,
as I in God's infinite spirals ascend.**

9. Serapis Bey, I consciously surrender all desires for the mechanical path of initiation created by the false hierarchy. I surrender the dream that by fulfilling certain outer requirements, I can automatically acquire a title or certain abilities.

Accelerate into Purity, I AM real,
Accelerate into Purity, all life heal,
Accelerate into Purity, I AM MORE,
Accelerate into Purity, all will soar.

Accelerate into Purity! (3X)
Beloved Elohim Astrea.
Accelerate into Purity! (3X)
Beloved Gabriel and Hope.
Accelerate into Purity! (3X)
Beloved Serapis Bey.
Accelerate into Purity! (3X)
Beloved I AM.

## Part 2

1. Serapis Bey, I consciously surrender all desires for attaining mastery over matter without having purified the self and thereby attained self-mastery.

> Gabriel Archangel, your light I revere,
> immersed in your Presence, nothing I fear.
> A disciple of Christ, I do leave behind,
> the ego's desire for responding in kind.
>
> **Gabriel Archangel, of this I am sure,**
> **Gabriel Archangel, Christ light is the cure.**
> **Gabriel Archangel, intentions so pure,**
> **Gabriel Archangel, in you I'm secure.**

2. Serapis Bey, I consciously surrender the dream of the fallen beings. I am willing to purify the self in order to attain true self-mastery.

> Gabriel Archangel, I fear not the light,
> in purifications' fire, I delight.
> With your hand in mine, each challenge I face,
> I follow the spiral to infinite grace.
>
> **Gabriel Archangel, of this I am sure,**
> **Gabriel Archangel, Christ light is the cure.**
> **Gabriel Archangel, intentions so pure,**
> **Gabriel Archangel, in you I'm secure.**

3. Serapis Bey, I consciously surrender all desires for attaining self-mastery through control of the self.

## 5 | Invoking the Power of Intention

> Gabriel Archangel, your fire burning white,
> ascending with you, out of the night.
> My ego has nowhere to run and to hide,
> in ascension's bright spiral, with you I abide.

> **Gabriel Archangel, of this I am sure,**
> **Gabriel Archangel, Christ light is the cure.**
> **Gabriel Archangel, intentions so pure,**
> **Gabriel Archangel, in you I'm secure.**

4. Serapis Bey, I consciously surrender the image that you are a strict disciplinarian. I surrender the illusion that if I follow your rules and endure your discipline, then I will be able to control the self.

> Gabriel Archangel, your trumpet I hear,
> announcing the birth of Christ drawing near.
> In lightness of being, I now am reborn,
> rising with Christ on bright Easter morn.

> **Gabriel Archangel, of this I am sure,**
> **Gabriel Archangel, Christ light is the cure.**
> **Gabriel Archangel, intentions so pure,**
> **Gabriel Archangel, in you I'm secure.**

5. Serapis Bey, I consciously surrender all desires for controlling the self by forcing my body and outer mind to live up to a set of outer rules and standards.

> Michael Archangel, in your flame so blue,
> there is no more night, there is only you.
> In oneness with you, I am filled with your light,
> what glorious wonder, revealed to my sight.

**Michael Archangel, your Faith is so strong,**
**Michael Archangel, oh sweep me along.**
**Michael Archangel, I'm singing your song,**
**Michael Archangel, with you I belong.**

6. Serapis Bey, I consciously surrender all desires for hiding anything from you, including the intentions in my subconscious mind. I am willing to have you show me the impurities that hide the subconscious mind.

Michael Archangel, protection you give,
within your blue shield, I ever shall live.
Sealed from all creatures, roaming the night,
I remain in your sphere, of electric blue light.

**Michael Archangel, your Faith is so strong,**
**Michael Archangel, oh sweep me along.**
**Michael Archangel, I'm singing your song,**
**Michael Archangel, with you I belong.**

7. Serapis Bey, I am willing to submit myself to your initiations and have you look at every level of my mind. I am willing to look at anything that you want to show me about myself.

Michael Archangel, what power you bring,
as millions of angels, praises will sing.
Consuming the demons, of doubt and of fear,
I know that your Presence, will always be near.

**Michael Archangel, your Faith is so strong,**
**Michael Archangel, oh sweep me along.**
**Michael Archangel, I'm singing your song,**
**Michael Archangel, with you I belong.**

8. Serapis Bey, I consciously surrender all desires for claiming that I want to follow the initiations of the Fourth Ray under Serapis Bey, while at the same time having something I want to hide from you.

> Michael Archangel, God's will is your love,
> you bring to us all, God's light from Above
> God's will is to see, all life taking flight,
> transcendence of self, our most sacred right.
>
> **Michael Archangel, your Faith is so strong,**
> **Michael Archangel, oh sweep me along.**
> **Michael Archangel, I'm singing your song,**
> **Michael Archangel, with you I belong.**

9. Serapis Bey, I consciously surrender all desires from the fallen consciousness for getting rid of something without seeing the impurity.

> With angels I soar,
> as I reach for MORE.
> The angels so real,
> their love all will heal.
> The angels bring peace,
> all conflicts will cease.
> With angels of light,
> we soar to new height.
>
> **The rustling sound of angel wings,**
> **what joy as even matter sings,**
> **what joy as every atom rings,**
> **in harmony with angel wings.**

## Part 3

1. Serapis Bey, I consciously surrender all desires to avoid facing God or the spiritual teacher from the ascended realm. I am willing to purify my consciousness of all of the things that magnetize me to the material realm.

> Serapis Bey, what power lies,
> behind your purifying eyes.
> Serapis Bey, it is a treat,
> to enter your sublime retreat.

> **O Holy Spirit, flow through me,**
> **I am the open door for thee.**
> **O mighty rushing stream of Light,**
> **transcendence is my sacred right.**

2. Serapis Bey, I consciously surrender all desires for forcing my way into heaven by hiding something from the ascended masters.

> Serapis Bey, what wisdom found,
> your words are always most profound.
> Serapis Bey, I tell you true,
> my mind has room for naught but you.

> **O Holy Spirit, flow through me,**
> **I am the open door for thee.**
> **O mighty rushing stream of Light,**
> **transcendence is my sacred right.**

## 5 | Invoking the Power of Intention

3. Serapis Bey, I consciously surrender all desires for cheating on the path of initiation by hiding my true intentions from you.

> Serapis Bey, what love beyond,
> my heart does leap, as I respond.
> Serapis Bey, your life a poem,
> that calls me to my starry home.

> **O Holy Spirit, flow through me,**
> **I am the open door for thee.**
> **O mighty rushing stream of Light,**
> **transcendence is my sacred right.**

4. Serapis Bey, I consciously surrender all desires for owning something and wanting to bring it with me into the ascended state.

> Serapis Bey, your guidance sure,
> my base is clear and white and pure.
> Serapis Bey, no longer trapped,
> by soul in which my self was wrapped.

> **O Holy Spirit, flow through me,**
> **I am the open door for thee.**
> **O mighty rushing stream of Light,**
> **transcendence is my sacred right.**

5. Serapis Bey, I consciously surrender all desires for passing the initiations in your retreat while hiding something from myself.

Serapis Bey, what healing balm,
in mind that is forever calm.
Serapis Bey, my thoughts are pure,
your discipline I shall endure.

**O Holy Spirit, flow through me,
I am the open door for thee.
O mighty rushing stream of Light,
transcendence is my sacred right.**

6. Serapis Bey, I consciously surrender all desires for controlling the self by suppressing the elements of the self that are not acceptable according to an outer standard.

Serapis Bey, what secret test,
for egos who want to be best.
Serapis Bey, expose in me,
all that is less than harmony.

**O Holy Spirit, flow through me,
I am the open door for thee.
O mighty rushing stream of Light,
transcendence is my sacred right.**

7. Serapis Bey, I consciously surrender all desires for making it through your retreat while carrying my impurities with me. I am willing to have you show me the beliefs behind all of my impurities.

Serapis Bey, what moving sight,
my self ascends to sacred height.
Serapis Bey, forever free,
in sacred synchronicity.

## 5 | Invoking the Power of Intention

> **O Holy Spirit, flow through me,**
> **I am the open door for thee.**
> **O mighty rushing stream of Light,**
> **transcendence is my sacred right.**

8. Serapis Bey, I consciously surrender all desire to exercise power for the purpose of control, the desire to attain power in order to be able to control my situation.

> Serapis Bey, you balance all,
> the seven rays upon my call.
> Serapis Bey, in space and time,
> the pyramid of self, I climb.

> **O Holy Spirit, flow through me,**
> **I am the open door for thee.**
> **O mighty rushing stream of Light,**
> **transcendence is my sacred right.**

9. Serapis Bey, I consciously surrender all desires for producing a state of mind, all desires for changing my inner situation by exercising control of my outer situation.

> Serapis Bey, your Presence here,
> filling up my inner sphere.
> Life is now a sacred flow,
> God Purity I do bestow.

> **O Holy Spirit, flow through me,**
> **I am the open door for thee.**
> **O mighty rushing stream of Light,**
> **transcendence is my sacred right.**

## Part 4

1. Serapis Bey, I consciously surrender all desires for having physical power without having the purity of intention. I am willing to have you help me purify my intention by exposing to me all hidden and impure motives.

> Master MORE, come to the fore,
> I will absorb your flame of MORE.
> Master MORE, my will so strong,
> my power center cleared by song.

> **O Holy Spirit, flow through me,**
> **I am the open door for thee.**
> **O mighty rushing stream of Light,**
> **transcendence is my sacred right.**

2. Serapis Bey, I consciously surrender all desires for attaining special powers, even the Gifts of the Holy Spirit, in order to demonstrate and prove something and thereby convert millions of people.

> Master MORE, your wisdom flows,
> as my attunement ever grows.
> Master MORE, we have a tie,
> that helps me see through Serpent's lie.

> **O Holy Spirit, flow through me,**
> **I am the open door for thee.**
> **O mighty rushing stream of Light,**
> **transcendence is my sacred right.**

## 5 | Invoking the Power of Intention

3. Serapis Bey, I consciously surrender all desires for dominating or controlling other people and matter in order to make myself feel a certain way. My intention is to master the self, not by controlling the self but by *mastering* the self.

> Master MORE, your love so pink,
> there is no purer love, I think.
> Master MORE, you set me free,
> from all conditionality.

**O Holy Spirit, flow through me,
I am the open door for thee.
O mighty rushing stream of Light,
transcendence is my sacred right.**

4. Serapis Bey, I am willing to attain self-mastery by looking at all of the impurities in my consciousness and consciously letting them go and deciding on a higher intention.

> Master MORE, I will endure,
> your discipline that makes me pure.
> Master MORE, intentions true,
> as I am always one with you.

**O Holy Spirit, flow through me,
I am the open door for thee.
O mighty rushing stream of Light,
transcendence is my sacred right.**

5. Serapis Bey, I consciously surrender all desires that are out of alignment with the intentions of the ascended masters. I am willing to tune in to your intentions.

Master MORE, my vision raised,
the will of God is always praised.
Master MORE, creative will,
raising all life higher still.

**O Holy Spirit, flow through me,
I am the open door for thee.
O mighty rushing stream of Light,
transcendence is my sacred right.**

6. Serapis Bey, I am willing to use conscious willpower to bring myself beyond the ego's intentions for exercising power. I am accelerating myself to the intention that you demonstrate to me.

Master MORE, your peace is power,
the demons of war it will devour.
Master MORE, we serve all life,
our flames consuming war and strife.

**O Holy Spirit, flow through me,
I am the open door for thee.
O mighty rushing stream of Light,
transcendence is my sacred right.**

7. Serapis Bey, I consciously surrender all desires for demonstrating some kind of mastery by being more powerful, richer or more beautiful than others. I am following a higher, non-dualistic vision.

> Master MORE, I am so free,
> eternal bond from you to me.
> Master MORE, I find rebirth,
> in flow of your eternal mirth.
>
> **O Holy Spirit, flow through me,
> I am the open door for thee.
> O mighty rushing stream of Light,
> transcendence is my sacred right.**

8. Serapis Bey, I consciously surrender all desires for the experience of being able to control others or control matter without looking at myself. I surrender the desire for using other people or external circumstances as an excuse for not looking at myself.

> Master MORE, you balance all,
> the seven rays upon my call.
> Master MORE, forever MORE,
> I am the Spirit's open door.
>
> **O Holy Spirit, flow through me,
> I am the open door for thee.
> O mighty rushing stream of Light,
> transcendence is my sacred right.**

9. Serapis Bey, I see the purpose of the initiations you offer at your retreat, and I am willing to embark upon your path. I am ready for what you offer, and I am willing to have you help me open my eyes.

Master MORE, your Presence here,
filling up my inner sphere.
Life is now a sacred flow,
God Power I on all bestow.

**O Holy Spirit, flow through me,
I am the open door for thee.
O mighty rushing stream of Light,
transcendence is my sacred right.**

## *Sealing:*

In the name of the Divine Mother, I fully accept that the power of these calls is used to set free the Ma-ter light, so it can outpicture the perfect vision of Christ for my own life, for all people and for the planet. In the name I AM THAT I AM, it is done! Amen.

# 6 | PURE INTENTIONS FOR SEEKING WISDOM

I am the Ascended Master Serapis Bey. The purpose of this discourse is to give to your outer awareness some pointers that will help you tune in to and pass the initiations on the second level at my retreat at Luxor. This, of course, is the level of the Second Ray, the ray of wisdom. We have already gone through important insights and initiations under Lord Lanto but I aim to take them a bit further by linking wisdom to your intention, the purity of your intention for seeking wisdom.

I would like you to consider how the world looks at wisdom. There was a time, many centuries and even millennia ago, where wisdom was looked at differently than it is today. You, who have grown up in the modern world, can scarcely imagine how people of ancient times looked at wisdom. I am not thereby saying that their approach to wisdom was necessarily superior to what can be achieved today. I *am* saying that it was certainly more nuanced and in a sense also a deeper understanding of wisdom than what you have in most of the educational establishments in the modern world.

## Limits to human knowledge

Back then, people realized that there was a limit to human knowledge. This was, of course, easier for them because human knowledge was much more limited back then than it is today. You have grown up in a world where there is an information explosion. Never has there been so much knowledge available to all human beings on earth. Well, actually, when I say "never," I mean according to your recorded history, for surely in past ages there were civilizations where even more knowledge was available than today. In what you call history, you live in a society where there is so much wisdom, so much knowledge, available that you cannot comprehend it all. There is no one who can know everything.

Back in ancient times, where there was less knowledge available, people realized that the only way to truly be successful in life was not through outer knowledge but through an inner wisdom. This was a higher form of wisdom that came in the form of what you today call intuition, but which back then they used different names for than you use today. They saw it as guidance from Above. Some cultures saw this as spiritual teachers, as spirit guides, some as a higher part of your own being. They realized that there was a higher form of knowledge or wisdom than what the human mind itself could produce.

There were also other cultures and other time periods where there was more of an understanding of what we might call the wisdom of the Mother, the feminine wisdom. This is the knowledge of how the world works, how the universe works. There were many people who had achieved a greater intuitive understanding for how the world works than even your scientists have today. I am not saying that this was a superior form of wisdom necessarily, although in some cases there were people who knew intuitively how the world works beyond what even your best scientists can do today. For example, there were people who had a better intuitive understanding of the human body and could therefore perform certain acts of healing that were beyond what the best doctors can do today. What they could not do back then was explain how and why these cures worked, and this, of course, is one difference and one area where today you have made a certain amount of progress. It is not my intention here to say that the immense explosion of knowledge created by science over the last several centuries is primitive or wrong.

## Self-mastery and knowledge from within

I do aim to help you, as an ascended master student engaging in the path of self-mastery, to see that you are not going to attain self-mastery through knowledge that comes to you from without. If you will look at society as it is today and how it looks at wisdom or knowledge, you will see that there is a clear tendency to think that reliable knowledge can only come from some kind of expert, some kind of authority figure.

There are still societies where they look to religious authorities to tell you what is the only way to believe about certain aspects of life. These religious authorities supposedly base this on their knowledge of the scriptures or in certain cases on some Divine revelation. There are other areas of society where they look to scientists to provide reliable knowledge.

Now again, science has made great progress in explaining many things about how the material universe works. However, as a spiritual student you need to realize that the approach taken by modern science is very limited. It is limited precisely because at a very early stage science became a tool for certain fallen beings who attempted to use it. First, they attempted to use it as a way to take the same power in society that other fallen beings had taken through religion. The warfare between science and religion is, therefore, to a large extent the rivalry between two groups of fallen beings.

After they had taken some of the power away from religion, the fallen beings who are using science now started using it as a way to control people. You may think that the fallen beings have many reasons for wanting to control people and, yes there *are* different levels of fallen beings and they have different motivations for why they want to control people. Behind them all, there is one overall desire when it comes to people who are in embodiment on earth, and that desire is that the fallen beings want to make sure that you cannot manifest personal Christhood.

Personal Christhood is, of course, a state where you know from within what is valid knowledge and what is not valid knowledge. You are self-sufficient, you are independent, there is no authority figure, there is no expert, who can tell you something that will override what you know from within. Christhood is the combination of the ability to receive knowledge from a higher source – namely your I AM Presence and the ascended masters – and the ability to tune in to the material universe and the wisdom of the Mother.

## The fascination with intellectual knowledge

When you come to the second level of initiation at my retreat, I need to exert a considerable effort to help the students overcome their fixation, their fascination, with outer, intellectual, scientific knowledge. This I do in various ways, but I do it primarily by taking the students into a room specially constructed for this purpose. This is a room that I have constructed with

## 6 | Pure Intentions for Seeking Wisdom

the help of Lord Lanto. It is a room where we can, as Lanto has described in his retreat, show the energy of wisdom, the energy of knowledge. We can show the geometric forms behind what you call outer knowledge, meaning knowledge that can be expressed in words.

We can therefore show you what is the energy behind worldly knowledge. We can even show you how there are certain ideas, certain types of knowledge, that are not neutral. You will know that the Holy Grail of scientific materialism has, for a couple of centuries, been objectivity. This is supposedly where the mind of the scientist does not influence the observations. It is believed that the conclusions drawn based on those observations are not influenced by the mind of the scientist.

It is therefore believed that scientific knowledge is completely neutral. It aims only to give you the truth; it has no other agenda or effect. We can, however, show you at an energetic level how there are some theories in the world, even some that are commonly believed by most people, that have certain energetic hooks embedded within them.

I know this is difficult to visualize, but it is not so difficult when you compare it to the world of computers. You know very well that a computer program has a certain code. It is coded in the language used for that particular computer. The computer program may contain information that it can give to you but the information is encoded. You also know that it is possible, between or inside a computer code, to insert hidden codes that are called viruses. These are codes that can go into your computer and perform various actions that have nothing to do with the outer program that they are riding on. You can have a situation where one thing is displayed on your computer screen, but at the same time there is a hidden virus that is doing something that you are not aware of. Well, it is the same with these ideas and theories created by the fallen beings. They all have outer knowledge that they claim have a certain aim, a certain theory, a certain intent of explaining how reality works. Hidden within it are encoded ideas, even energetic signals, that are not seen by the conscious mind, but they go into the subconscious mind and act as a computer virus.

All of you, who have been brought up in the modern world, have been programmed with certain ideas that at the surface level claim to give you knowledge – valid, neutral, objective knowledge – but that are in reality programming your minds in certain ways that work against your spiritual growth and the manifestation of your Christhood. There are many examples of this. I do not here intend to go into a longer discourse about it because this is the work of many ascended masters for another time. What I do aim to show you is just an example of what you will learn at my retreat.

## The problem with the theory of evolution

One of the most common ideas that are out there in the world is, of course, the idea of evolution. It is portrayed by materialistic science that the current theory of evolution, which goes back to Charles Darwin, is presenting you an objective view of how life originated and how it has reached its current level. This is, of course, an entirely materialistic theory. It has been one of the primary weapons used against religion, and it has caused many people to abandon all belief in religion and spirituality, accepting that human beings are entirely material beings.

This, of course, is not an idea that you can use to attain your Christhood. You cannot believe that you are nothing more than an evolved animal and at the same time walk the spiritual path and aim for a state of mind that is so far beyond what any human being or any evolved animal could ever attain. The theory of evolution in its current form promotes this view of yourself that is in direct antithesis to the development of your Christhood. We can show you this on a screen of how the beliefs in the mental body, that are inserted by the theory of evolution, actually block your access to your identity body.

You understand, my beloved, that in order to develop your Christhood, you have to work on all of your four lower bodies. You do have to purify your physical body of certain toxins and you have to give up certain habits. You cannot develop Christhood if you are smoking, taking recreational drugs of any kind or drinking alcohol. It cannot be done because the physical body will block your access to your three higher bodies.

At the same time, you need to work on your emotional body in order to purify it of certain emotional energies. You cannot develop Christhood if you are mortally afraid of everything in this world, thinking you live in a universe that is out to get you, or even if you are afraid of the power elite and thinking there is some hidden conspiracy that is out to get you. You cannot develop Christhood if you are consumed by anger or hatred against other people and want revenge because then your emotional body will block your conscious access to the beliefs in your mental body.

Likewise, there are beliefs in your mental body that will block your access to the identity body. If you cannot change your identity consciously, how can you develop Christhood? Christhood is about shifting your sense of identity so you identify yourself as a son or daughter of God, as an extension of the ascended hierarchy above you and as an extension of your I AM Presence.

What did Jesus say? "I can of my own self do nothing, the Father within me, he doeth the work." Well, if you cannot purify your identity body of the sense that you are a human being, then how can you let the Father within you work through you? It cannot be done.

## Ideas that block Christhood

Most people have been programmed with a set of ideas that are in direct opposition to their spiritual growth. I, of course, need to challenge some of these ideas, but it is not my role, at my level of initiation, to challenge all of them. What I *will* do, however, is to challenge your motivation for seeking wisdom. Of course, when I say that certain ideas have a virus embedded within them, we might say that all of the knowledge that has come out of materialistic science has a virus embedded within it because materialistic science presents itself as having a monopoly on truth, on reliable knowledge.

Only that which has been proven or measured by materialistic science is considered valid knowledge. This, of course, you cannot believe, you cannot accept, if you are to develop a pure motivation for seeking wisdom. What is it that materialism programs people to do? Well, it programs them to seek a specific kind of knowledge. Not only is this materialistic knowledge, it is by its very nature knowledge that does not reach beyond a certain level. It is not living wisdom. With "living wisdom," I mean knowledge that is based on the realization of how the world truly works.

Materialistic knowledge says that the material universe is a self-contained unit. There is nothing outside the material universe. Therefore, there is no source of energy that is sending energy into the material universe. This, of course, is in complete opposition to the reality of how the universe works. The universe is constantly being upheld, and it is growing, because there is a stream of energy flowing from the ascended realm into the four levels of the material universe. If this stream stopped today, the material universe as you know it would very quickly start deteriorating.

You, as a spiritual student, absolutely need to overcome this belief. You may say: "But Serapis Bey, how could I have worked through the first books in this series if I did not believe that there are ascended masters who live in another realm and that you can send us energy?" Yes, my beloved, of course you believe this with your outer minds. When you come to the second level of initiation at my retreat, it is time to show you that despite what you believe with your outer minds, there are still certain beliefs, certain viruses, that have been embedded in your emotional, mental and identity bodies. These will to some degree block your walk towards self-mastery. They will also block or distort your motivation for seeking knowledge.

## *The dream of secret knowledge*

So many students engage in our course towards self-mastery with a motivation for seeking knowledge that is not pure and not constructive. I have already talked about the people who are seeking to overpower others. There are many, many students, as Lanto also mentioned, that seek knowledge in order to compete with others and prove their superiority. This is not my primary concern, as those who have passed the initiations under Lanto have turned this corner. My concern is that there are many students who are still believing that it is possible to find some secret knowledge, some secret wisdom, some secret formula that will give them mechanical control over matter, their own situation or even other people.

There are people in the world, my beloved, who are open to a spiritual approach to life but who are seeking certain spells or incantations that can get another person to fall in love with them. Now, how people can believe that magically forcing another person to fall in love with them will be real love is a topic I will not go into here, but you see the point, do you not? There are many, many people who still believe that the purpose of walking the spiritual path is to gradually receive some secret knowledge or formula that will give you mechanical control. This is *not* the case.

Yes, my beloved, there is certain knowledge, there are certain formulas, that have been developed by the fallen beings over a very long period of time. It is possible to obtain this knowledge and these formulas, and it is possible thereby to have a certain control of mind over matter. This is *not* the path of the ascended masters; this is the path of the false hierarchy.

## How the earth is different from the original version

You may already be beginning to realize that I will be talking, in this book, about the contrast between the ascended masters and the false hierarchy, for it is on the 4th ray that you need to accelerate yourself beyond the reach of the false hierarchy. I ask you to listen very carefully and to read these passages over and over again until your conscious mind begins to fully grasp what I am saying.

You are living in an unascended sphere. An unascended sphere does not function as the ascended realm. As you will know, if you have studied a broad selection of our teachings, an unascended sphere functions as a realm in which beings can exercise their free will with a considerable degree of latitude as to what they can do with that free will. The inhabitants of a planet like earth have been allowed to develop, to manifest, many conditions that are very, very far from what is present in the ascended realm. I am sure you can see that war is not a condition found in the ascended realm. What is war, if not an extreme example of how far certain beings will go in order to attain power and control over human beings? If you read Mother Mary's book on war (*Help the Ascended Masters Stop War*), you will see exactly how far the fallen beings will go.

What I am pointing out to you here is that conditions on earth are presently at a very low level compared to the ascended realm. This means that there are certain, what we might call "secondary," laws of nature that are in effect on earth. You have certain primary laws of nature that are functioning based on the vision of the Elohim.

You understand that when the Elohim created the earth, or for that matter the entire material universe, they defined certain laws of nature that are, so to speak, holding the universe together, holding matter together, allowing there to be matter structures, such as planets or your physical bodies. These are what I call the primary laws of nature.

Because the inhabitants of earth have free will, they actually have the ability to create certain conditions that are not in direct opposition to the primary laws of nature but that are, so to speak, existing in a gray zone. They are allowed to exist in an imperfect state because the earth is a teaching device for those who will not listen to direct knowledge from the ascended masters. On earth they can manifest certain conditions that are expressions of their own consciousness. The purpose is, of course, to give people a certain experience until they have had enough of it and want something higher.

This caused the original inhabitants of the earth to develop certain limiting conditions on earth, to manifest a certain downward spiral where they were not transcending themselves. This was, as we have explained, what caused those who oversee the evolution of earth to allow certain fallen beings to embody here. Some of these fallen beings had fallen in a previous sphere and had therefore had a very long time to develop a certain mastery over matter. When they came to earth, they took those abilities with them. They built on to the downward spiral created by the original inhabitants of earth. They, so to speak, expanded or accelerated it in a downward direction.

## The secondary laws of nature

This has caused all of the inhabitants of the earth to collectively create certain conditions. For example, matter is more dense today than it was when the earth was created by the Elohim. This also means that your physical bodies are more dense today than the original bodies of the first inhabitants of this planet. Homo sapiens is not a pure creation of the Elohim but a modified version of the original pure bodies created by the Elohim. Your bodies are more dense and that is why they are susceptible to certain diseases.

Matter is more dense, that is why you have to work harder to manifest what you need for your bodies to survive. The denser bodies need to take in more dense nourishment, which can only be achieved from a more dense form of matter. The more dense the matter, the more work it requires to change it. That is why so many people have lost the ability to change matter through the mind and must therefore change matter through their physical bodies that have the same density as matter.

Currently, on planet earth there are certain secondary laws of nature that are not the original laws defined by the Elohim. These laws have actually been defined by the collective consciousness of humanity—of course under the hidden guidance of the fallen beings. There are secondary laws of nature that you can use to create a certain wisdom, a certain formula, a certain form of what we call black magic that will give you some control over matter in an almost mechanical way. I say in an almost mechanical way because it is not entirely mechanical. There is no truly mechanical way to control matter unless you do it through physical means.

What modern technology, material technology, is aimed at doing is giving you mechanical control over matter, over nature. This can be done at the physical level, but it cannot be done in an entirely mechanical way at the level of the mind. You cannot come up with a formula that can be used by the mind or that can be spoken as an incantation, a curse or a magical formula that is entirely mechanical. You can, however, create certain formulas that will allow certain people to have some degree of control over matter, but it is not entirely mechanical. It still requires some flow of energy from the spiritual realm.

## *Why fallen beings don't have complete control*

This actually means that the fallen beings cannot exercise completely mechanical control through the secondary laws of nature, through their formulas that make use of these laws. Why can't they do this? Because a fallen being who has fallen in a previous sphere, or fallen below a certain level of consciousness, cannot access the flow of energy from the spiritual realm. What do the fallen beings then need to do? They need to get that energy by stealing it from other people, people who still have some flow of energy through their beings.

That is why you see the very old matrix of a wizard taking on an apprentice. The wizard is supposedly teaching the apprentice all of his tricks, but he is also stealing the energy of the apprentice and using it to perform those tricks. Some of the fallen beings can use many people to steal energy and thereby perform certain feats. There are many ways in which the fallen beings can do this, many tricks they have developed. The point here is this: It is possible for you, as a spiritual student, to find certain knowledge, certain "wisdom," we might call it in quotation marks, certain formulas and incantations that can give you a certain control over matter.

There are those out there in the world today who have set themselves up as gurus or spiritual teachers and who claim they can give you such control over matter. Some will even claim that they can do this in a faster way than the ascended masters can do so, that they have a shortcut. Well, it may shock you to hear that they are actually right. They do have a shortcut! There are things you can do to develop a certain mastery over matter without walking the path of self-mastery.

## Ascended masters do not teach magic

As I said in my last discourse: If this is the experience you desire to have, then by all means go after it. You are free to leave the door to my retreat at any time, but you need to know with absolute certainty that I, Serapis Bey, will not give you that experience. I will not give you a shortcut. I will not give you a secret formula.

What I *will* do is help you walk the path of self-mastery where you accelerate your mind beyond the secondary laws of nature to where you can begin to use the primary laws defined by the Elohim. This is the goal of this course of self-mastery, not a shortcut through the black magic developed by the fallen beings.

Speaking of black magic, there is, of course, a concept in the world that calls itself "white magic." They claim to also have a shortcut, to also have certain formulas, certain wisdom, that can give you control over matter, but they claim this is entirely benign.

Well, my beloved—again: If this is the experience you desire, you need to leave my retreat in order to get it. The ascended masters are not about black magic or white magic or any other form of magic. Saint Germain has talked about "eye magic" but that is said almost jokingly, for truly there is no magic.

We are not teaching you a kind of magic that works in mysterious ways or that gives you mechanical control. We are teaching you self-mastery. What did I say in my first discourse? You cannot pass the initiations on the first level of my retreat if your focus is on changing other people or conditions outside yourself rather than changing yourself.

On the second level of initiation your focus needs to be on seeking knowledge for the purpose of changing yourself, not for the purpose of changing other people or external conditions. The knowledge that you need to seek in order to pass the initiations at my retreat, and in order to pass the initiations on the three higher rays, is self-knowledge.

## Why you need self-knowledge

This is not an outer self-knowledge of how you can again create some kind of shortcut or control yourself. It is a matter of purifying your mind from all imperfect forms of knowledge about yourself. What is the knowledge, the wisdom, that you need to seek at this level? It is not knowledge about how to do something *outside* the self. It is not knowledge about how to do something *inside* the self. It is the knowledge that allows you to see the impurities in the self so that you can consciously surrender them, let them go, replace them with a higher decision, a higher form of wisdom and insight. This is not a matter of analyzing yourself, it is not a matter of intellectualizing or making long lists of your beliefs. It is a matter of tuning in to a higher source of wisdom.

Ultimately, that source is your I AM Presence, but given that you are at my retreat, then at this level of initiation I am that source. I do not aim to give you outer wisdom. I do not have classes at the second level where I stand on the podium or at the blackboard and give knowledge to the students. I teach in only one way: I sit.

Some of you will find it difficult to envision Serapis Bey sitting, but I am, of course, capable of doing so. I sit in front of the students, or rather I sit in a position and the students sit in a circle around me. Then, I have the students go through an exercise of seeking to tune out everything but my Presence. As the line in my decree says: "My mind has room for naught but you."

In the beginning, this is, of course, impossible for the students. Their minds are constantly pulled here or there, often by the knowledge, the wisdom, they have taken in. They start thinking, going off on a tangent. As the students work with me and with the other instructors at my retreat, they begin to purify their minds of this worldly wisdom, these false ideas, these impure intentions for seeking wisdom.

## Seeking wisdom that is not useful

Then, they face a second level of initiation because what does it take to tune in to my Presence? It takes that you have no intention of gaining any form of knowledge that you consider useful or valuable. If you will think about this, you will see that most people have the idea that wisdom must be useful. It must be something that you can use to do something or at least to know something that you did not know before. This is not what I am asking you to do. I am asking you to tune in to my Presence with no intention of gaining knowledge that is useful or valuable, with no intention of getting knowledge that can be put on a scale of more or less.

Your intention must be to tune in to my Presence and to experience my Presence—nothing else. You may say: "But we are in an etheric retreat." You are free from the constraints of the physical body, but you are not free from the constraints of your emotional, mental and identity bodies. Until you reach a certain purity of intention in those three bodies, you will not actually be able to tune in.

How do we determine who among a group of students can tune in to my Presence? It is very simple. We go into a room that is shielded from any outside influence. There is therefore nothing coming from the outside that disturbs the students. I sit, the students sit in a circle. I ask them to do the etheric equivalent of closing their eyes, meaning focusing within, and then tune in to my Presence, which is very close to them. After a certain time, there will be someone who opens the equivalent of a door and gently calls the students to come outside. Those students who have not tuned in to my Presence, will leave. Those students who *have* tuned in to my Presence, will not even hear the call to leave.

In the beginning, all of the students will hear the call and will leave. As time goes on, some will hear the call but will not leave because they want to stay and tune in to my Presence. After more time has passed, some will not even hear the call and we now know that they have reached the level where they are not seeking wisdom in order to use it for something in the world. They are seeking it for one purpose only and that is because they have realized that true self-mastery means coming into oneness with the spiritual hierarchy of which you are a part. The first step in being a co-creator and exercising your mastery over matter is to tune in to the Presence of the master who is above you in hierarchy. It is from there that the energy that drives your creative effort comes.

This is the accelerated form of wisdom that you need to tune in to at the second level of my retreat. You can even do this from your waking awareness. You can do it by contemplating all of the different motives that pull you away from simply tuning in. You can do it by giving my decree or the invocation for this lesson and then setting aside some time to sit quietly with no other aim than to tune in to my Presence. You may not be successful in experiencing my Presence through the density of the physical body, but let not this discourage you. Making the effort is in itself worth it.

Even if you have no conscious awareness of my Presence, the intent and the effort will have an effect that will help you pass the initiation at the etheric level, at the level of my retreat. The outer goes hand in hand with the inner so I encourage you to give the invocation based on this discourse and after that take some time to tune in to my Presence. Do this after each invocation you give, as you use the rest of this book, and you may be surprised at the results.

Serapis Bey I AM. My Presence is here for you only, if you will but attune to it with no other intention than just experiencing the Presence that I AM.

# 7 | INVOKING WISE INTENTIONS

In the name I AM THAT I AM, Jesus Christ, I call to my I AM Presence to flow through the I Will Be Presence that I AM and give this invocation with full power. I call to beloved Elohim Purity and Astrea and Apollo and Lumina, Archangel Gabriel and Hope and Jophiel and Christine, Serapis Bey and Lord Lanto to help me transcend all false motives for seeking wisdom. Help me see and surrender all patterns that block my oneness with Serapis Bey and with my I AM Presence, including …

[Make personal calls]

## Part 1

1. Serapis Bey, I consciously surrender all desires for being successful by acquiring outer knowledge, intellectual knowledge.

Beloved Astrea, your heart is so true,
your Circle and Sword of white and blue,
cut all life free from dramas unwise,
on wings of Purity our planet will rise.

**Beloved Astrea, in God Purity,**
**accelerate all of my life energy,**
**raising my mind into true unity**
**with the Masters of love in Infinity.**

2. Serapis Bey, I am seeking inner wisdom, guidance from above and the wisdom of the Mother, the feminine wisdom.

Beloved Astrea, from Purity's Ray,
send forth deliverance to all life today,
acceleration to Purity, I AM now free
from all that is less than love's Purity.

**Beloved Astrea, in oneness with you,**
**your circle and sword of electric blue,**
**with Purity's Light cutting right through,**
**raising within me all that is true.**

3. Serapis Bey, I consciously surrender all desires for attaining self-mastery through knowledge that comes to me from without.

Beloved Astrea, accelerate us all,
as for your deliverance I fervently call,
set all life free from vision impure
beyond fear and doubt, I AM rising for sure.

## 7 | Invoking Wise Intentions

> Beloved Astrea, I AM willing to see,
> all of the lies that keep me unfree,
> I AM rising beyond every impurity,
> with Purity's Light forever in me.

4. Serapis Bey, I consciously surrender the belief that reliable knowledge can only come from some expert or authority figure, be it a religious, political or scientific authority.

> Beloved Astrea, accelerate life
> beyond all duality's struggle and strife,
> consume all division between God and man,
> accelerate fulfillment of God's perfect plan.

> **Beloved Astrea, I lovingly call,**
> **break down separation's invisible wall,**
> **I surrender all lies causing the fall,**
> **forever affirming the oneness of All.**

5. Serapis Bey, I consciously desire personal Christhood, the state where I know from within what is valid knowledge and what is not valid knowledge.

> Beloved Apollo, with your second ray,
> you open my eyes to see a new day,
> I see through duality's lies and deceit,
> transcending the mindset producing defeat.

> **Beloved Apollo, thou Elohim Gold,**
> **your radiant light my eyes now behold,**
> **as pages of wisdom you gently unfold,**
> **I feel I am free from all that is old.**

6. Serapis Bey, I consciously strive to be self-sufficient and independent. I will not let any authority figure tell me something that will override what I know from within.

> Beloved Apollo, in your flame I know,
> that your living wisdom is always a flow,
> in your light I see my own highest will,
> immersed in the stream that never stands still.

> **Beloved Apollo, your light makes it clear,**
> **why we have taken embodiment here,**
> **working to raise our own cosmic sphere,**
> **together we form the tip of the spear.**

7. Serapis Bey, I am consciously striving for the ability to receive knowledge from a higher source, namely my I AM Presence and the ascended masters, and the ability to tune in to the material universe and the wisdom of the Mother.

> Beloved Apollo, exposing all lies,
> I hereby surrender all ego-based ties,
> I know my perception is truly the key,
> to transcending the serpentine duality.

> **Beloved Apollo, we heed now your call,**
> **drawing us into Wisdom's Great Hall,**
> **exposing all lies causing the fall,**
> **you help us reclaim the oneness of all.**

8. Serapis Bey, I consciously surrender all fixation on, all fascination with, outer, intellectual, scientific knowledge. Show me the theories that have energetic hooks embedded within them.

Beloved Apollo, your wisdom so clear,
in oneness with you, no serpent I fear,
the beam in my eye I'm willing to see,
I'm free from the serpent's own duality.

**Beloved Apollo, my eyes now I raise,
I see that the Earth is in a new phase,
I willingly stand in your piercing gaze,
empowered, I exit duality's maze.**

9. Serapis Bey, expose to me any beliefs I have that are based on the ideas and theories created by the fallen beings, the ideas that contain energetic signals that go into the subconscious mind and act as a computer virus.

Accelerate into Purity, I AM real,
Accelerate into Purity, all life heal,
Accelerate into Purity, I AM MORE,
Accelerate into Purity, all will soar.

Accelerate into Purity! (3X)
Beloved Elohim Astrea.
Accelerate into Purity! (3X)
Beloved Gabriel and Hope.
Accelerate into Purity! (3X)
Beloved Serapis Bey.
Accelerate into Purity! (3X)
Beloved I AM.

## Part 2

1. Serapis Bey, I consciously surrender the belief that I am nothing more than an evolved animal. I see that it is a direct antithesis to the development of my Christhood.

> Gabriel Archangel, your light I revere,
> immersed in your Presence, nothing I fear.
> A disciple of Christ, I do leave behind,
> the ego's desire for responding in kind.

> **Gabriel Archangel, of this I am sure,**
> **Gabriel Archangel, Christ light is the cure.**
> **Gabriel Archangel, intentions so pure,**
> **Gabriel Archangel, in you I'm secure.**

2. Serapis Bey, I consciously acknowledge that Christhood is about shifting my sense of identity so I identify myself as an extension of the ascended hierarchy above me and as an extension of my I AM Presence.

> Gabriel Archangel, I fear not the light,
> in purifications' fire, I delight.
> With your hand in mine, each challenge I face,
> I follow the spiral to infinite grace.

> **Gabriel Archangel, of this I am sure,**
> **Gabriel Archangel, Christ light is the cure.**
> **Gabriel Archangel, intentions so pure,**
> **Gabriel Archangel, in you I'm secure.**

# 7 | Invoking Wise Intentions

3. Serapis Bey, I consciously surrender the belief that materialistic science can give me all of the knowledge I need. I desire living wisdom, knowledge that is based on the realization of how the world truly works.

> Gabriel Archangel, your fire burning white,
> ascending with you, out of the night.
> My ego has nowhere to run and to hide,
> in ascension's bright spiral, with you I abide.
>
> **Gabriel Archangel, of this I am sure,**
> **Gabriel Archangel, Christ light is the cure.**
> **Gabriel Archangel, intentions so pure,**
> **Gabriel Archangel, in you I'm secure.**

4. Serapis Bey, I am willing to work with you on clearing the beliefs, the viruses, that have been embedded in my emotional, mental and identity bodies in order to distort my motivation for seeking knowledge.

> Gabriel Archangel, your trumpet I hear,
> announcing the birth of Christ drawing near.
> In lightness of being, I now am reborn,
> rising with Christ on bright Easter morn.
>
> **Gabriel Archangel, of this I am sure,**
> **Gabriel Archangel, Christ light is the cure.**
> **Gabriel Archangel, intentions so pure,**
> **Gabriel Archangel, in you I'm secure.**

5. Serapis Bey, I consciously surrender all desires for finding some secret knowledge, wisdom or formula that will give me mechanical control over matter, my own situation or other people.

> Jophiel Archangel, in wisdom's great light,
> all serpentine lies exposed to my sight.
> So subtle the lies that creep through the mind,
> yet you are the greatest teacher I find.

> **Jophiel Archangel, exposing all lies,**
> **Jophiel Archangel, cutting all ties.**
> **Jophiel Archangel, clearing the skies,**
> **Jophiel Archangel, my mind truly flies.**

6. Serapis Bey, I consciously surrender all desires for following the fallen beings and acquiring their knowledge and formulas for controlling matter.

> Jophiel Archangel, your wisdom I hail,
> your sword cutting through duality's veil.
> As you show the way, I know what is real,
> from serpentine doubt, I instantly heal.

> **Jophiel Archangel, exposing all lies,**
> **Jophiel Archangel, cutting all ties.**
> **Jophiel Archangel, clearing the skies,**
> **Jophiel Archangel, my mind truly flies.**

7. Serapis Bey, I am consciously deciding that I want to follow the path of the ascended masters; not the path of the false hierarchy.

# 7 | Invoking Wise Intentions

Jophiel Archangel, your reality,
the best antidote to duality.
No lie can remain in your Presence so clear,
with you on my side, no serpent I fear.

**Jophiel Archangel, exposing all lies,
Jophiel Archangel, cutting all ties.
Jophiel Archangel, clearing the skies,
Jophiel Archangel, my mind truly flies.**

8. Serapis Bey, I consciously surrender all desires for manipulating the secondary laws of nature that are defined by the collective consciousness of humanity under the guidance of the fallen beings.

Jophiel Archangel, God's mind is in me,
and through your clear light, its wisdom I see.
Divisions all vanish, as I see the One,
and truly, the wholeness of mind I have won.

**Jophiel Archangel, exposing all lies,
Jophiel Archangel, cutting all ties.
Jophiel Archangel, clearing the skies,
Jophiel Archangel, my mind truly flies.**

9. Serapis Bey, I consciously surrender all desires for learning the wisdom, formulas or black magic that will give me some control over matter in a mechanical way.

With angels I soar,
as I reach for MORE.
The angels so real,
their love all will heal.
The angels bring peace,
all conflicts will cease.
With angels of light,
we soar to new height.

**The rustling sound of angel wings,
what joy as even matter sings,
what joy as every atom rings,
in harmony with angel wings.**

## Part 3

1. Serapis Bey, I consciously surrender all desires for being the apprentice of a wizard who can teach me knowledge, wisdom or certain formulas and incantations that can give me control over matter.

Serapis Bey, what power lies,
behind your purifying eyes.
Serapis Bey, it is a treat,
to enter your sublime retreat.

**O Holy Spirit, flow through me,
I am the open door for thee.
O mighty rushing stream of Light,
transcendence is my sacred right.**

# 7 | Invoking Wise Intentions

2. Serapis Bey, I consciously surrender all desires for finding a faster way, a shortcut, for developing mastery over matter without walking the path of self-mastery.

> Serapis Bey, what wisdom found,
> your words are always most profound.
> Serapis Bey, I tell you true,
> my mind has room for naught but you.

**O Holy Spirit, flow through me,
I am the open door for thee.
O mighty rushing stream of Light,
transcendence is my sacred right.**

3. Serapis Bey, I am willing to walk the path of self-mastery where I accelerate my mind beyond the secondary laws of nature to where I can begin to use the primary laws defined by the Elohim.

> Serapis Bey, what love beyond,
> my heart does leap, as I respond.
> Serapis Bey, your life a poem,
> that calls me to my starry home.

**O Holy Spirit, flow through me,
I am the open door for thee.
O mighty rushing stream of Light,
transcendence is my sacred right.**

4. Serapis Bey, I consciously surrender all desires for learning white magic and the formulas that are supposedly benign.

Serapis Bey, your guidance sure,
my base is clear and white and pure.
Serapis Bey, no longer trapped,
by soul in which my self was wrapped.

**O Holy Spirit, flow through me,
I am the open door for thee.
O mighty rushing stream of Light,
transcendence is my sacred right.**

5. Serapis Bey, I consciously surrender all desires for seeking knowledge of how to change other people or conditions outside myself rather than changing myself.

Serapis Bey, what healing balm,
in mind that is forever calm.
Serapis Bey, my thoughts are pure,
your discipline I shall endure.

**O Holy Spirit, flow through me,
I am the open door for thee.
O mighty rushing stream of Light,
transcendence is my sacred right.**

6. Serapis Bey, I am consciously seeking knowledge for the purpose of changing myself. I am seeking the self-knowledge I need for passing the initiations at your retreat and on the three higher rays.

Serapis Bey, what secret test,
for egos who want to be best.
Serapis Bey, expose in me,
all that is less than harmony.

7 | *Invoking Wise Intentions*

> O Holy Spirit, flow through me,
> I am the open door for thee.
> O mighty rushing stream of Light,
> transcendence is my sacred right.

7. Serapis Bey, I consciously surrender all desires for finding outer self-knowledge of how I can create a shortcut for controlling myself.

> Serapis Bey, what moving sight,
> my self ascends to sacred height.
> Serapis Bey, forever free,
> in sacred synchronicity.

> O Holy Spirit, flow through me,
> I am the open door for thee.
> O mighty rushing stream of Light,
> transcendence is my sacred right.

8. Serapis Bey, I want your help in purifying my mind from all imperfect forms of knowledge about myself.

> Serapis Bey, you balance all,
> the seven rays upon my call.
> Serapis Bey, in space and time,
> the pyramid of self, I climb.

> O Holy Spirit, flow through me,
> I am the open door for thee.
> O mighty rushing stream of Light,
> transcendence is my sacred right.

9. Serapis Bey, I seek the knowledge that allows me to see the impurities in the self so that I can consciously surrender them and replace them with a higher decision, a higher form of wisdom and insight.

> Serapis Bey, your Presence here,
> filling up my inner sphere.
> Life is now a sacred flow,
> God Purity I do bestow.

> **O Holy Spirit, flow through me,**
> **I am the open door for thee.**
> **O mighty rushing stream of Light,**
> **transcendence is my sacred right.**

## Part 4

1. Serapis Bey, I consciously surrender all desires for analyzing myself, intellectualizing or making long lists of my beliefs. I am tuning in to a higher source of wisdom.

> Master Lanto, golden wise,
> expose in me the ego's lies.
> Master Lanto, will to be,
> I will to win my mastery.

> **O Holy Spirit, flow through me,**
> **I am the open door for thee.**
> **O mighty rushing stream of Light,**
> **transcendence is my sacred right.**

## 7 | Invoking Wise Intentions

2. Serapis Bey, I consciously accept you as my source for higher wisdom. I am seeking to tune out everything but your Presence.

> Master Lanto, balance all,
> for wisdom's balance I do call.
> Master Lanto, help me see,
> that balance is the Golden key.

> **O Holy Spirit, flow through me,**
> **I am the open door for thee.**
> **O mighty rushing stream of Light,**
> **transcendence is my sacred right.**

3. Serapis Bey, expose to me the outer knowledge, the wisdom, that causes my mind to be pulled away from attuning to your Presence.

> Master Lanto, from Above,
> I call forth discerning love.
> Master Lanto, love's not blind,
> through love, God vision I will find.

> **O Holy Spirit, flow through me,**
> **I am the open door for thee.**
> **O mighty rushing stream of Light,**
> **transcendence is my sacred right.**

4. Serapis Bey, help me purify my mind from all worldly wisdom, all false ideas, all impure intentions for seeking wisdom.

Master Lanto, pure I am,
intentions pure as Christic lamb.
Master Lanto, I will transcend,
acceleration now my truest friend.

**O Holy Spirit, flow through me,
I am the open door for thee.
O mighty rushing stream of Light,
transcendence is my sacred right.**

5. Serapis Bey, I consciously surrender all intention of gaining any form of knowledge that I consider useful or valuable. I surrender the idea that wisdom must be useful.

Master Lanto, I am whole,
no more division in my soul.
Master Lanto, healing flame,
all balance in your sacred name.

**O Holy Spirit, flow through me,
I am the open door for thee.
O mighty rushing stream of Light,
transcendence is my sacred right.**

6. Serapis Bey, I consciously surrender all intention of gaining knowledge that is useful or valuable, all intention of getting knowledge that can be put on a scale of more or less.

Master Lanto, serve all life,
as I transcend all inner strife.
Master Lanto, peace you give,
to all who want to truly live.

7 | *Invoking Wise Intentions*

> **O Holy Spirit, flow through me,**
> **I am the open door for thee.**
> **O mighty rushing stream of Light,**
> **transcendence is my sacred right.**

7. Serapis Bey, my sole intention is to tune in to your Presence and to experience your Presence—nothing else. Help me purify my emotional, mental and identity bodies and reach the purity of intention that enables me to tune in to your Presence.

> Master Lanto, free to be,
> in balanced creativity.
> Master Lanto, we employ,
> your balance as the key to joy.

> **O Holy Spirit, flow through me,**
> **I am the open door for thee.**
> **O mighty rushing stream of Light,**
> **transcendence is my sacred right.**

8. Serapis Bey, I consciously surrender all desires for seeking wisdom in order to use it for something in the world. I am seeking wisdom because I have realized that true self-mastery means coming into oneness with the spiritual hierarchy of which I am a part.

> Master Lanto, balance all,
> the seven rays upon my call.
> Master Lanto, I take flight,
> my threefold flame a blazing light.

> **O Holy Spirit, flow through me,**
> **I am the open door for thee.**
> **O mighty rushing stream of Light,**
> **transcendence is my sacred right.**

9. Serapis Bey, I consciously intend to tune in to the Presence of the master who is above me in hierarchy and from whom I receive the energy that drives my creative efforts. I desire to tune in to *you*.

> Lanto dear, your Presence here,
> filling up my inner sphere.
> Life is now a sacred flow,
> God Wisdom I on all bestow.

> **O Holy Spirit, flow through me,**
> **I am the open door for thee.**
> **O mighty rushing stream of Light,**
> **transcendence is my sacred right.**

## *Sealing:*

In the name of the Divine Mother, I fully accept that the power of these calls is used to set free the Ma-ter light, so it can outpicture the perfect vision of Christ for my own life, for all people and for the planet. In the name I AM THAT I AM, it is done! Amen.

# 8 | FROM FEAR-BASED TO LOVE-BASED INTENTIONS

I AM the Ascended Master Serapis Bey. What can you expect when you reach the third level at my retreat, the level where you encounter the combination of the Fourth Ray of Purity with the Third Ray of Love? You can, of course, expect to encounter my love.

This presents somewhat of a problem for some ascended master students who have come to see the Fourth Ray from a certain perspective and who have come to see me as a strict disciplinarian. As I have already said, I am not strict and I am not disciplining anyone. At the third level, those students who have not let go of this image of me, need to do so before they can really start the initiations of that level. I, of course, seek to help students do this, partly by talking to them, partly by demonstrating that I too am a master of love, as is each and every Chohan.

## Why we need not fear the masters

As we have said many times, you do not become an ascended master by having any kind of fear in your being. You become an ascended master by rising to a level of consciousness where you are the open door for the flow of love that comes from the ascended realm. There can be no fear in the mind of an ascended master.

There are, of course, many people on earth who fear encountering an ascended master or an angel. You may see in the Bible that in many cases where an angel appeared to someone, the angel would say: "fear not" because the people were in fear of anything out of the ordinary. There may be a fear among many ascended master students that you cannot hide anything from me. As I have said, when you are in my retreat, of course you cannot hide anything from me. Then again, if you are in my retreat intent on walking the path of initiation that I offer, why would you want to hide anything from me?

What I seek to demonstrate to you is that regardless of what I may see in your consciousness, I will still love you and I will still help you overcome that condition and move beyond it entirely. As I have said, the fourth level is the eye of the needle. The Fourth Ray represents the point on the course of self-mastery where you cannot go beyond until you purify your intention. When we say "purify your intention" we mean, of course, several things. The underlying need for purification is that you purify your intention of all fear-based intentions and raise yourself to a level where you only have love-based intentions left.

In order to do this, you must, of course, be willing to look at the fear-based intentions that you have. If you are afraid that I will condemn you if I see such intentions in you, then, of course, you cannot look at these. You will seek to hide them from yourself, thinking that if you can hide them from yourself, you can hide them from me also. This, naturally, is not the case. You can hide certain things from yourself, but you cannot hide them from me, for the simple reason that I have no fear in my being and therefore there is nothing behind which anything can be hidden.

## How fear hides things

You do see, do you not, that it is only fear that forms a barrier behind which things can be hidden? Why is it so that fear forms a barrier that can hide things? Well, in reality fear does not form a barrier, fear does not have any substance that can actually hide things. What fear does is that it makes you unwilling to look at something. Of course, when you are not willing to look at something, then that something is hidden to your conscious mind, is it not? There is no substance that can hide things from you if you are truly willing to look at it.

That is also why there is nothing to fear about looking at something in your own psychology. You will overcome the fear by looking at it. In fact, the only way to overcome the fear is to look at it, to look beyond what you fear to see that it is not nearly as bad as what you thought and that it cannot stop you from making progress on the path.

What the fallen beings have done is to give you the fear that if you look at certain things in your consciousness and see certain aspects of the fallen consciousness in your subconscious mind, then we of the ascended masters will reject you and you cannot go further on the path. Nothing is further from the truth. Where have we ever said that before you can become a student of the ascended masters, you need to have purified your consciousness from all impurities?

Think about it. I am the Chohan of the Fourth Ray of Purity. What is my role? It is to help students apply the Fourth Ray of Purity and use it to consume impurities. If you had no impurities, why would you need my help? My entire work as a Chohan is geared towards helping people overcome their impurities. How could I perform my work if I was constantly judging students and putting them down for having the impurities that I am here to help them overcome? It makes no sense when you think about it, but, of course, the fallen beings will try to prevent you from thinking about it and therefore hide behind the fear or seek to hide your impurities behind the fear.

You can, in fact, hide your impurities for the false teachers of the false hierarchy. The reason for this is that the false teachers also have fear in their beings. Therefore, what you cannot see, they in some cases cannot see either if they have not been willing to see it in themselves. I hope you realize that all fallen beings and false teachers have fear in their beings.

The more a being seems to have power and the ability to control, the more fear it has in its being. Why do you need to control? In order to be able to live with your fear! The greater the fear, the more you must exercise control in order to live with your fear. You need to ponder this with your conscious mind. You need to look at the world and see how some leaders throughout history, and even today, have, so to speak, ruled people with an iron fist, attempting to instill fear in their followers. They do this because they are afraid themselves.

Well, my beloved, when you are on the path to self-mastery, you cannot afford to fear someone in the material world or even in the three other octaves. If you are serious about following the ascended masters, you cannot allow yourself to also follow a fear-based teacher. As I have said before, there is nothing wrong with you deciding or realizing that you have a need to experience what it is like to follow a fear-based teacher from whom you can hide certain aspects of your subconscious.

If you need this experience, I will respect your free will, but then, of course, I cannot help you and so there is no point in you being in my retreat. However, I will not condemn you, I will not be angry with you. I will simply be ready to welcome you when you have had enough of the experience and want a love-based teacher. We of the ascended masters are entirely love-based teachers. We have no need to control you because we do not fear you or anything else.

## Discovering our fear-based intentions

Think about this very carefully because what I need you to do consciously, as you are following the initiations at the third level of my retreat in your finer bodies at night, is precisely to look at your life and look at the world and consider what intentions you have that are based on fear. If you look at the world today, you will see that the vast majority of the people have all of their intentions based on fear.

The fallen beings are very good at using the fear in themselves to control others. This we might say is one definition of a fallen being. I have said that many fallen beings have fallen from a previous sphere. This has in a certain sense taught them how to use fear, to use their own fear, to control others without overcoming their own fears. They still have the fears, but they have learned to use them to control others. They are, of course, also doing what I have talked about earlier: exercising a certain mastery of themselves by controlling themselves. This can give you some appearance of mastery, but it is not true self-mastery.

The fallen beings have been good at making you feel that you live in a world where there is something you need to fear. This fear takes innumerable forms. It is, of course, a fear that can be said to have a certain basis in the conditions you observe in the material realm on earth. As I said in my previous discourse, the fallen beings have defined certain secondary laws of nature because this is an unascended sphere. They have therefore defined certain laws and certain conditions that do present a difficulty, challenge, obstacle, opposition, threat, as it will be seen by most people. I am not trying to tell you, for example, that disease is not a reality, although a temporary one, on this planet. I am not telling you that the potential for war or conflict is not there or is not real.

What I *am* telling you is that the fallen beings have managed to get humankind to co-create the conditions that you see in the material universe. Then, the fallen beings have used those conditions to instill a fear in the population that causes most people to spend their entire lives acting based on fear-based intentions. Most people spend their entire energy seeking to somehow compensate for their fears, seeking to alleviate the fears so that they can live with them. This, of course, is, as the popular saying goes, not a way to live, at least not from the perspective of an ascended master.

It is, however, the way to live for people who have not taken responsibility for themselves and their own state of mind. They have a ready excuse in the conditions in the material universe for feeling that they do not need to look at their fears. They do not need to take responsibility, they do not need to accept that they have the power to raise themselves beyond, not only their fears but even the conditions that they fear. If you will not take responsibility for yourself, you need an excuse for not doing so. The fallen beings have supplied an almost endless number of such excuses through the fears of conditions in the material world. While you are going through the initiations on the third level of my retreat, and while you are giving these invocations every day, I need you to consciously look at your intentions. I need you to consider how many things you do and have done in your life that are aimed at either protecting yourself from certain conditions that you fear, compensating for such conditions or in other ways alleviating your fears of these conditions so that you can live with them.

I need you to, possibly, make a list. It can be a list in your head or it can be a written list; *that* I will leave up to you. You need to make some kind of list over what intentions you have acted upon in your life and that you are acting upon today that are based on fear. Then I need you to make another list of the intentions you either have or would like to have if you had no fears.

## Fear is caused by inner conditions

You understand that self-mastery cannot be achieved if your entire life is swallowed up in an attempt to protect yourself from or compensate for conditions in the material universe. Self-mastery cannot be attained if your entire inner life is aimed at compensating or alleviating the fears that you have. Self-mastery can be attained only by transcending the fears that you have.

Now, my beloved, I know that at this point many of my students face a particular problem that is to some degree created by the fallen beings or at least defined by them. Many students come to me, when we sit in groups at my retreat on the third level, and they say: "But Serapis Bey, we are still in physical embodiment. We understand that you, as an ascended master, do not fear the conditions on earth, such as war, disease or poverty. We understand this, but don't you see that we are still in embodiment and there is a risk that we could experience these conditions? We have thought that by attaining self-mastery, we would also attain the mastery of mind over matter so we could avoid these conditions in the physical realm, but we are realizing – and you are telling us – that we do not yet have this self-mastery and maybe we will not even have it when we complete the course. So how can we overcome the fear when we cannot change the physical conditions?"

My beloved, I fully understand why you face this seeming dilemma. I faced it myself when I was in embodiment, as has every ascended master. Yet I have ascended and so have many other masters from earth. How did I ascend? Because I realized that the key to overcoming fear is *not* to remove the outer conditions but to work on the fear directly within myself.

Fear is not caused by the outer condition. Fear is caused by an inner condition, by a certain decision in your mind. When you go into the duality consciousness, you go into the realm of fear. Fear is an inescapable companion of the consciousness of duality and separation. Why is this so? It is because the very nature of duality is that you have something that is reacting to you and to which you can then react again.

## Life as a tennis game

As I showed this messenger, life in the physical world can be compared to a tennis match. If you are standing on a tennis court with a racket and a set of balls, you can hit the ball across the net, but how many times can you do this when the ball is not coming back? What would you learn about the game of tennis if there was not a player on the other side who could send the ball back to you? Now, of course, you may choose not to go on the tennis court, but there is nothing wrong with walking onto the tennis court and saying: "I would like to experience the game of tennis, even attain some mastery in it." It is, despite all of the fear-based, epic mindset put out by the fallen beings, no more serious to go into duality than to play a game of tennis.

From a non-fear based viewpoint, duality is a game. It gives you a certain experience, you may attain a certain mastery in playing this game. Of course, from a non-fear based viewpoint, the purpose of playing the dualistic game is not to attain mastery of the game but to come to the point where it has given you a certain mastery of self so that you can now say: "I have had enough of this experience. It has taught me more about who I am and who I am not, and now I am ready to leave the game behind."

You need to begin to consciously ponder these ideas because surely one of the most subtle fears induced by the fallen beings is what we have called the epic mindset. It says that there is this epically important contest between the forces of light and the forces of darkness, and it has incredible significance what you do when you play this game, or rather when you engage in this supposed reality.

You need to come to a point where you realize that nothing that happens on earth has the significance claimed by the fallen beings. If you do not realize this, you will not be able to let go of the many subtle intentions that have been created by the fallen beings based on the idea of an epic battle between good and evil. I have said this before; I will say it again. It is not the goal of the ascended masters to have our students battle the fallen beings. It is not the goal of self-mastery to give you some ability whereby you can defeat the fallen beings and defeat the forces of darkness that are creating all kinds of evils on the earth. As long as you think that this is your goal, as long as your intention is to attain this kind of power to defeat the forces of darkness, your intention is based on fear.

You do not need to defeat the forces of darkness, you need to bring the light. You cannot be the open door for the light as long as there is fear in your being and an unwillingness to look at the conditions in your own mind. How do you ultimately overcome the fear of certain conditions on earth? You do not overcome it by changing those conditions, by eradicating them or by protecting yourself from them. Any protection that you seek on earth, any material protection, becomes your prison. This is not the case for spiritual protection, but it is the case for physical protection.

The noblemen of the Middle Ages who sat in their fortified castles were trapped in those castles. Those who wore a suit of armor were protected but were also trapped inside a tin can, and I can assure you it was a rather unpleasant experience. You do not overcome fear by removing the condition you fear. You overcome fear only by going into the fear, seeing that it has no reality, seeing the decision you made that made you believe it had reality and then undoing that condition.

## Fear-based intentions cannot overcome fear

Here, my beloved, is the essential realization: Overcoming fear cannot be done with a motivation based on fear. If your intention is based on fear, you cannot overcome the fear. Therefore, you are facing what again seems like a dilemma, a catch-22. It is, of course, only a dilemma when looked at from a state of fear.

That is why the initiations you face at the third level of my retreat are aimed at helping you develop a loved-based intention. You can help yourself by pondering this with your conscious mind. We are doing many things at this level that are aimed at helping you overcome the fear in your identity body, your mental body and your emotional body. You can complete this only by also looking at the fear with your conscious mind.

What you can do is realize what I have said, namely that the goal is to overcome fear, but you cannot do it if your intention is based on fear. You must develop a conscious intention based on love. This you do by pondering what it is that really brought you to my retreat, that really brought you to the spiritual path and this course. When you make a list of your fear-based intentions, you may see that there are certain of these intentions that drove you to follow the spiritual path. Most students have certain fear-based intentions for following the path. You seek to escape something. You seek to compensate for your own mistakes of the past or your own perceived inadequacies and imperfections. You seek to make yourself so perfect that God simply has to accept you into the kingdom, even though you have not really changed your state of consciousness, your sense of self.

When you make a list of these intentions, and you see that they are fear-based, something will dawn on you. You will realize that even though these intentions do influence your path, they cannot completely explain why you are walking the spiritual path and why you have reached the point where you are studying this book. You could not have walked through the initiations of the first three rays and reached the initiations of the Fourth Ray if your intention was entirely based on fear. It simply is not possible.

Your fear would have long ago caused you to reject this course or to say: "I will take a break and continue it later" (the "later" that never comes). You will, when you ponder this, discover that there is something you love about the spiritual path, about the ascended masters, about the ascended realm, about the idea of self-transcendence, the idea of walking the path. There is something you love and that something becomes the fixed point for you overcoming your fears.

## Love is your fixed point

You may have heard that one of the fathers of geometry, the Greek philosopher Archimedes said: "Give me a fixed point and a lever and I will move the universe." Well, in an unascended sphere that is still affected by fear, there is only one fixed point and it is love. When you have love, you can move the universe. Now, I realize that at your present level you may not have the sufficient intensity and concentration of love to move the universe. I am not asking you to move the universe, I am only asking you to move the very next fear you are facing right now. Then, of course, I will be asking you to remove the next, but I will only ask you to remove what you are capable of removing at your present level.

This is what I do when you attend my retreat in your finer bodies. If you will attune to it with your conscious mind, then most of you will be able to consciously realize what fear you are working on. You can then look at it, you can go into it, with me holding your hand if you like, and you can see the unreality behind it.

Take note, again, that there may be a condition on earth that is real in a temporary sense. I am not asking you see the unreality of that condition, I am asking you to see the unreality of your fear of that condition. I know very well that there are many conditions on earth that seem very threatening. You may be exposed to a war and you may be killed. You may contract a deadly disease and die. Your body will eventually grow old and die. Sure, you cannot change these conditions, but what I am asking you to do is to realize that you do not need to change these conditions.

Your ascension and your spiritual progress does not depend on you changing any condition outside yourself. It depends on one thing only, namely that you realize that no condition in the material universe can define you as a spiritual being.

This is one of the most subtle effects of what the fallen beings have done. So many people on earth believe that material conditions define them, define what kind of beings they are and what they can and what they *especially* cannot do. Therefore, you think that if you are affected by a disease, killed in a war or die of old age this will define you and prevent you from making spiritual progress.

## Overcoming the fear of death

There are many people who have lived their whole lives in fear of a certain condition, for example death. Then, on their deathbed, they have suddenly realized that there was nothing to fear because death is not the end, they will live on. I assume you realize that you will live on after death and that you have died many times in previous lifetimes. Have you actually fully realized with your conscious mind that death cannot stop your spiritual progress or your ascension?

If you believe that Jesus ascended and that he died on the cross, then you see, right there, that death, physical death, does not prevent you from ascending. Therefore, you know that it does not prevent you from learning certain lessons and growing. No matter what condition you might face on this earth, no matter how terrible, no matter how much suffering and pain it might cause you, it cannot define you, stop your growth or prevent your ascension.

Many people have had to face a certain condition in order to overcome their fear of the condition. My aim with this course, and the aim of the other Chohans, is of course to get you to the point where you can overcome your fear of physical conditions without facing and experiencing those conditions. We do not want you to live the rest of your life in the fear of death and only overcome it on your deathbed. We want you to overcome it right now so that you can live the rest of your life without fearing death, without fearing disease, without fearing war or any of the other conditions you might fear.

## Overriding the laws of nature

This is what I seek to achieve at the third level of my retreat. Why is this so important? Because the aim of our course in self-mastery is, as I have explained, to help you master the primary laws of nature defined by the Elohim. These laws can override the secondary laws of nature defined by the fallen beings.

You saw Jesus perform what has been called miracles. They were not miracles. Jesus appeared in a society and a time where everybody was so trapped in fear that their minds and their bodies had become subject to the secondary laws of nature. These laws were seemingly insurmountable obstacles to these people. Jesus demonstrated that when you attain the Christ consciousness, you can begin to make use of the primary laws of nature and these can override, set aside, neutralize the secondary laws.

Our goal is to help you master the primary laws and actually transcend not only the fear of the secondary laws but even the desire to master those laws. As I have said, you can attain some mastery of the secondary laws. This is what the false hierarchy will teach you. I do not teach this and neither do the other Chohans.

This also means that you do not indiscriminately use the primary laws of nature to override the secondary laws. You will see that Jesus did not heal every sick person he encountered. He did not raise from the dead every person that died in his nearness. He did not turn all the water into wine. He did not walk on water every other day. He did this only to demonstrate what is possible when you switch the mind from the fear-based state of mind to the love-based state of mind. Thereby, you attain the ability to transcend and no longer be bound by the secondary laws of nature but instead become an open door for the primary laws of nature to work through you.

## Becoming neutral

It is the same with you. We cannot help you complete this course if you form an intention of wanting to master the primary laws in order to impress other people or demonstrate anything to them. You understand that when Jesus performed his so-called miracles, he did not decide with his outer mind: "I am going to heal that person." Jesus was completely neutral.

He was the open door so that the hierarchy above him could act through him and decide whether a person should be healed or not. Jesus, of course, said: "He who believes on me shall do the works that I did." We intend to take you to a point where you can do the works that Jesus did, but this does not mean that the Spirit will do the same works through you as it did through Jesus. This is something that will be decided by the Spirit based on an individual evaluation of the actual situation.

You, therefore, cannot become an open door if you have an intention of what Spirit should or should not do. I realize that you cannot fully overcome this intention at this level. I want you to be aware of it so that you may keep it somewhere in the back of your mind. There will come a point later on the path where this will be precisely the intention you need to overcome in order to move forward.

Again, we are not aiming to produce particular outer results on earth. Yes, Saint Germain has a plan for manifesting a golden age on earth, but it is not a plan that is laid out in every detail. There is much room for the Spirit to work and for free will to outplay itself. There is a general intention and that is how love-based intention is. Love-based intention is not a straitjacket. I have said that you need to bring yourself into alignment with the hierarchy above you, but this does not mean that you lose your free will and individual creativity.

When you are in alignment with the Spirit, there are certain things you would never even think about doing or desire to do. Within a general framework of your own Divine plan and what is needed in the moment, you still have room to exercise creativity and to make decisions. This is a necessary understanding to reach, for if you fear that you will give up your freedom, your free will and creativity by walking the path and completing this course, then that is another fear-based intention that will hold you back.

It is not that you will give up your free will. It is that your will actually becomes free because you no longer have a fear-based intention programmed into your subconscious mind by the fallen beings whereby they can control you and control the choices you make, even the choices you can see, the options you can see.

# 8 | From Fear-Based to Love-Based Intentions

## *Creativity is not compensating for lack*

How do the fallen beings control people? By limiting the options they can see, by making you think that certain things are impossible or are not allowed. By making you think that it is impossible or un-allowed for you to manifest and express your Christhood or by making you think that you do not want it because it is putting on a straitjacket.

"Intention…intention…intention." Intention that is based on love sets your will free from all fear. It also sets your creativity free so you are truly creative in seeing a higher vision and manifesting it rather than compensating for the conditions, the lack, that you currently see on earth. I agree with you that there are many things on earth that are not ideal and that ideally could be changed. You may be here to bring about certain change on earth, but the change you are here to bring about is not a reaction to the current imperfect conditions. The true change, the true creativity, is to bring forth something that is so new that it replaces conditions that are currently here.

I talked about the tennis game where you have an opponent that is sending something back to you. Well, this is one function of the fallen beings. They form the opponent to those people who are not as aggressive. Of course, *you* also form their opponent and give them an opportunity to have had enough of the game.

They are the opponent for you as long as you are playing the game and trapped in duality, as long as you think that your intention as a spiritual student should be to be able to correct, to change, to eradicate the current limitations on earth, to remove the evil from earth. This is not your true goal. Your true love-based intention is to demonstrate that there is an alternative to the dualistic state of consciousness.

Why is it that modern technology cannot solve all problems? Why is it that the current approach to medicine cannot cure all diseases? It is because it is fear-based, aiming at changing the conditions that spring from duality rather than bringing a new approach that looks at the problem from a love-based frame of mind and therefore brings forth a solution that does not compensate for the limitations but transcends them completely.

I have given you many things to ponder in this lesson, but I have not given you more than it is possible for you to deal with at this level of initiation. If you are on the fast track of using nine days for each lesson, you may want to go a little further on the initiation of love. You may want to spend a little more time pondering your intentions because it will help you more easily pass the initiation of the fourth level where you get a double dose of purity. It is very difficult to handle a double dose of purity if you do not have an entirely love-based intention.

Serapis Bey I AM.

# 9 | INVOKING LOVE-BASED INTENTIONS

In the name I AM THAT I AM, Jesus Christ, I call to my I AM Presence to flow through the I Will Be Presence that I AM and give this invocation with full power. I call to beloved Elohim Purity and Astrea and Heros and Amora, Archangel Gabriel and Hope and Chamuel and Charity, Serapis Bey and Paul the Venetian to help me transcend all fear-based intentions and develop and discover my love-based intentions. Help me see and surrender all patterns that block my oneness with Serapis Bey and with my I AM Presence, including …

[Make personal calls]

## Part 1

1. Serapis Bey, I am willing to encounter your love. I consciously surrender the image of you as a strict disciplinarian.

Beloved Astrea, your heart is so true,
your Circle and Sword of white and blue,
cut all life free from dramas unwise,
on wings of Purity our planet will rise.

**Beloved Astrea, in God Purity,**
**accelerate all of my life energy,**
**raising my mind into true unity**
**with the Masters of love in Infinity.**

2. Serapis Bey, I know you are a master of love because one becomes an ascended master by rising to a level of consciousness where one is the open door for the flow of love that comes from the ascended realm.

Beloved Astrea, from Purity's Ray,
send forth deliverance to all life today,
acceleration to Purity, I AM now free
from all that is less than love's Purity.

**Beloved Astrea, in oneness with you,**
**your circle and sword of electric blue,**
**with Purity's Light cutting right through,**
**raising within me all that is true.**

3. Serapis Bey, I consciously surrender all desires for hiding anything from you. I am consciously deciding that I do not fear you or fear having you show me what I need to transcend.

Beloved Astrea, accelerate us all,
as for your deliverance I fervently call,
set all life free from vision impure
beyond fear and doubt, I AM rising for sure.

# 9 | Invoking Love-Based Intentions

**Beloved Astrea, I AM willing to see,
all of the lies that keep me unfree,
I AM rising beyond every impurity,
with Purity's Light forever in me.**

4. Serapis Bey, I consciously know that regardless of what you may see in my consciousness, you will still love me. You will still help me overcome that condition and move beyond it entirely.

Beloved Astrea, accelerate life
beyond all duality's struggle and strife,
consume all division between God and man,
accelerate fulfillment of God's perfect plan.

**Beloved Astrea, I lovingly call,
break down separation's invisible wall,
I surrender all lies causing the fall,
forever affirming the oneness of All.**

5. Serapis Bey, I am willing to let go of all fear-based intentions and raise myself to a level where I only have love-based intentions left. I am willing to look at the fear-based intentions I have.

O Heros-Amora, in your love so pink,
I care not what others about me may think,
in oneness with you, I claim a new day,
an innocent child, I frolic and play.

**O Heros-Amora, a new life begun,
I laugh at the devil, the serious one,
I bathe in your glorious Ruby-Pink Sun,
knowing my God allows life to be fun.**

6. Serapis Bey, I consciously surrender the fear that you will condemn me if you see such intentions in me. I do not want to hide anything from you or from myself.

O Heros-Amora, life is such a joy,
I see that the world is like a great toy,
whatever my mind into it projects,
the mirror of life exactly reflects.

**O Heros-Amora, I reap what I sow,
yet this is Plan B for helping me grow,
for truly, Plan A is that I join the flow,
immersed in the Infinite Love you bestow.**

7. Serapis Bey, I consciously see that it is only fear that forms a barrier behind which things can be hidden. I am willing to look at anything that is hidden to my conscious mind.

O Heros-Amora, conditions you burn,
I know I AM free to take a new turn,
Immersed in the stream of infinite Love,
I know that my Spirit came from Above.

**O Heros-Amora, awakened I see,
in true love is no conditionality,
the devil is stuck in his duality,
but I AM set free by Love's reality.**

8. Serapis Bey, I consciously see that there is nothing to fear about looking at something in my own psychology. I will overcome the fear by looking at it and seeing that it cannot stop me from making progress on the path.

> O Heros-Amora, I feel that at last,
> I've risen above the trap of my past,
> in true love I claim my freedom to grow,
> forever I'm one with Love's Infinite Flow.

> **O Heros-Amora, conditions are ties,**
> **forming a net of serpentine lies,**
> **your love has no bounds, forever it flies,**
> **raising all life into Ruby-Pink skies.**

9. Serapis Bey, I consciously surrender the fear that if I look at certain things in my consciousness, and see certain aspects of the fallen consciousness, then you will reject me and I cannot go further on the path.

> Accelerate into Purity, I AM real,
> Accelerate into Purity, all life heal,
> Accelerate into Purity, I AM MORE,
> Accelerate into Purity, all will soar.

> Accelerate into Purity! (3X)
> Beloved Elohim Astrea.
> Accelerate into Purity! (3X)
> Beloved Gabriel and Hope.
> Accelerate into Purity! (3X)
> Beloved Serapis Bey.
> Accelerate into Purity! (3X)
> Beloved I AM.

## Part 2

1. Serapis Bey, I consciously see that as the Chohan of the Fourth Ray of Purity, it is your role to help me apply the Fourth Ray and use it to consume impurities. If I had no impurities, why would I need your help?

> Gabriel Archangel, your light I revere,
> immersed in your Presence, nothing I fear.
> A disciple of Christ, I do leave behind,
> the ego's desire for responding in kind.
>
> **Gabriel Archangel, of this I am sure,**
> **Gabriel Archangel, Christ light is the cure.**
> **Gabriel Archangel, intentions so pure,**
> **Gabriel Archangel, in you I'm secure.**

2. Serapis Bey, I consciously see that your entire work as a Chohan is geared towards helping me overcome my impurities. You are not judging me for having the impurities that you are here to help me overcome.

> Gabriel Archangel, I fear not the light,
> in purifications' fire, I delight.
> With your hand in mine, each challenge I face,
> I follow the spiral to infinite grace.
>
> **Gabriel Archangel, of this I am sure,**
> **Gabriel Archangel, Christ light is the cure.**
> **Gabriel Archangel, intentions so pure,**
> **Gabriel Archangel, in you I'm secure.**

## 9 | Invoking Love-Based Intentions

3. Serapis Bey, I consciously surrender all desires to have a teacher from whom I can hide my impurities. I surrender all desire to follow the false hierarchy who have fear in their beings.

> Gabriel Archangel, your fire burning white,
> ascending with you, out of the night.
> My ego has nowhere to run and to hide,
> in ascension's bright spiral, with you I abide.
>
> **Gabriel Archangel, of this I am sure,**
> **Gabriel Archangel, Christ light is the cure.**
> **Gabriel Archangel, intentions so pure,**
> **Gabriel Archangel, in you I'm secure.**

4. Serapis Bey, I consciously see that the more a being seems to have power and the ability to control, the more fear it has in its being. We need to control in order to be able to live with our fear.

> Gabriel Archangel, your trumpet I hear,
> announcing the birth of Christ drawing near.
> In lightness of being, I now am reborn,
> rising with Christ on bright Easter morn.
>
> **Gabriel Archangel, of this I am sure,**
> **Gabriel Archangel, Christ light is the cure.**
> **Gabriel Archangel, intentions so pure,**
> **Gabriel Archangel, in you I'm secure.**

5. Serapis Bey, I consciously surrender all fear of anyone in the material world or the three higher octaves. I surrender any attachment to any fear-based teacher.

Chamuel Archangel, in ruby ray power,
I know I am taking a life-giving shower.
Love burning away all perversions of will,
I suddenly feel my desires falling still.

**Chamuel Archangel, descend from Above,**
**Chamuel Archangel, with ruby-pink love,**
**Chamuel Archangel, so often thought-of,**
**Chamuel Archangel, o come Holy Dove.**

6. Serapis Bey, I am willing to have you show me what intentions I have that are based on fear. Show me how the fallen beings have used fear to control me.

Chamuel Archangel, a spiral of light,
as ruby ray fire now pierces the night.
All forces of darkness consumed by your fire,
consuming all those who will not rise higher.

**Chamuel Archangel, descend from Above,**
**Chamuel Archangel, with ruby-pink love,**
**Chamuel Archangel, so often thought-of,**
**Chamuel Archangel, o come Holy Dove.**

7. Serapis Bey, I consciously see that the fallen beings have managed to get humankind to co-create the conditions in the material universe. They have used those conditions to instill a fear in the population that causes most people to spend their entire lives acting on fear-based intentions.

> Chamuel Archangel, your love so immense,
> with clarified vision, my life now makes sense.
> The purpose of life you so clearly reveal,
> immersed in your love, God's oneness I feel.
>
> **Chamuel Archangel, descend from Above,**
> **Chamuel Archangel, with ruby-pink love,**
> **Chamuel Archangel, so often thought-of,**
> **Chamuel Archangel, o come Holy Dove.**

8. Serapis Bey, I consciously decide that I no longer want to be controlled by fear-based intentions. I am willing to take responsibility for myself and my own state of mind.

> Chamuel Archangel, what calmness you bring,
> I see now that even death has no sting.
> For truly, in love there can be no decay,
> as love is transcendence into a new day.
>
> **Chamuel Archangel, descend from Above,**
> **Chamuel Archangel, with ruby-pink love,**
> **Chamuel Archangel, so often thought-of,**
> **Chamuel Archangel, o come Holy Dove.**

9. Serapis Bey, I consciously decide that I am willing to look at my intentions. Show me how many things I do and have done in my life that are aimed at either protecting myself from certain conditions, compensating for such conditions or alleviating my fears of these conditions so I can live with the fear.

With angels I soar,
as I reach for MORE.
The angels so real,
their love all will heal.
The angels bring peace,
all conflicts will cease.
With angels of light,
we soar to new height.

**The rustling sound of angel wings,**
**what joy as even matter sings,**
**what joy as every atom rings,**
**in harmony with angel wings.**

## Part 3

1. Serapis Bey, help me see what intentions I have acted upon, and that I am acting upon today, that are based on fear. Help me see the intentions I either have or would like to have if I had no fears.

Serapis Bey, what power lies,
behind your purifying eyes.
Serapis Bey, it is a treat,
to enter your sublime retreat.

**O Holy Spirit, flow through me,**
**I am the open door for thee.**
**O mighty rushing stream of Light,**
**transcendence is my sacred right.**

## 9 | Invoking Love-Based Intentions

2. Serapis Bey, I consciously realize that I do not overcome fear by removing the outer conditions but by working on the fear directly within myself. Fear is not caused by the outer condition but by an inner condition. It is an inescapable consequence of going into duality.

> Serapis Bey, what wisdom found,
> your words are always most profound.
> Serapis Bey, I tell you true,
> my mind has room for naught but you.
>
> **O Holy Spirit, flow through me,**
> **I am the open door for thee.**
> **O mighty rushing stream of Light,**
> **transcendence is my sacred right.**

3. Serapis Bey, I consciously see that, despite all of the fear-based, epic mindset put out by the fallen beings, it is no more serious to go into duality than to play a game of tennis.

> Serapis Bey, what love beyond,
> my heart does leap, as I respond.
> Serapis Bey, your life a poem,
> that calls me to my starry home.
>
> **O Holy Spirit, flow through me,**
> **I am the open door for thee.**
> **O mighty rushing stream of Light,**
> **transcendence is my sacred right.**

4. Serapis Bey, I consciously see that duality is a game. I consciously say: "I have had enough of this experience. It has taught me more about who I am and who I am not, and now I am ready to leave the game behind."

> Serapis Bey, your guidance sure,
> my base is clear and white and pure.
> Serapis Bey, no longer trapped,
> by soul in which my self was wrapped.

> **O Holy Spirit, flow through me,**
> **I am the open door for thee.**
> **O mighty rushing stream of Light,**
> **transcendence is my sacred right.**

5. Serapis Bey, I consciously see that nothing that happens on earth has the significance claimed by the fallen beings. I hereby let go of the many subtle intentions that have been created by the fallen beings based on the idea of an epic battle between good and evil.

> Serapis Bey, what healing balm,
> in mind that is forever calm.
> Serapis Bey, my thoughts are pure,
> your discipline I shall endure.

> **O Holy Spirit, flow through me,**
> **I am the open door for thee.**
> **O mighty rushing stream of Light,**
> **transcendence is my sacred right.**

6. Serapis Bey, I consciously surrender all desires to battle the fallen beings. I surrender the desire to have an ability whereby I can defeat the fallen beings and the forces of darkness that are creating all kinds of evils on the earth.

> Serapis Bey, what secret test,
> for egos who want to be best.
> Serapis Bey, expose in me,
> all that is less than harmony.

**O Holy Spirit, flow through me,
I am the open door for thee.
O mighty rushing stream of Light,
transcendence is my sacred right.**

7. Serapis Bey, I consciously see that I do not need to defeat the forces of darkness, I need to bring the light. I surrender all desires for defeating darkness or protecting myself through material means.

> Serapis Bey, what moving sight,
> my self ascends to sacred height.
> Serapis Bey, forever free,
> in sacred synchronicity.

**O Holy Spirit, flow through me,
I am the open door for thee.
O mighty rushing stream of Light,
transcendence is my sacred right.**

8. Serapis Bey, I consciously see the essential realization that overcoming fear cannot be done with a motivation based on fear. Help me develop a loved-based intention and help me look at my fear with my conscious mind.

> Serapis Bey, you balance all,
> the seven rays upon my call.
> Serapis Bey, in space and time,
> the pyramid of self, I climb.

> **O Holy Spirit, flow through me,**
> **I am the open door for thee.**
> **O mighty rushing stream of Light,**
> **transcendence is my sacred right.**

9. Serapis Bey, I consciously surrender all desires for making myself so perfect that God simply has to accept me into the kingdom, even though I have not really changed my state of consciousness and sense of self.

> Serapis Bey, your Presence here,
> filling up my inner sphere.
> Life is now a sacred flow,
> God Purity I do bestow.

> **O Holy Spirit, flow through me,**
> **I am the open door for thee.**
> **O mighty rushing stream of Light,**
> **transcendence is my sacred right.**

## 9 | Invoking Love-Based Intentions

## Part 4

1. Serapis Bey, I consciously see that my fear-based intentions cannot completely explain why I am walking the spiritual path. Behind all fear, I do have love-based intentions and these are my fixed point for lifting myself out of fear.

> Master Paul, venetian dream,
> your love for beauty's flowing stream.
> Master Paul, in love's own womb,
> your power shatters ego's tomb.

> **O Holy Spirit, flow through me,**
> **I am the open door for thee.**
> **O mighty rushing stream of Light,**
> **transcendence is my sacred right.**

2. Serapis Bey, I am willing to attune to you with my conscious mind. Help me consciously realize what fear I am working on, and I *will* look at it. I will go into it, with you holding my hand, so I can see the unreality behind it.

> Master Paul, your counsel wise,
> my mind is raised to lofty skies.
> Master Paul, in wisdom's love,
> such beauty flowing from Above.

> **O Holy Spirit, flow through me,**
> **I am the open door for thee.**
> **O mighty rushing stream of Light,**
> **transcendence is my sacred right.**

3. Serapis Bey, I consciously see that there are conditions on earth that are real in a temporary sense. You are not asking me to see the unreality of such conditions, but to see the unreality of my fear of such conditions.

> Master Paul, love is an art,
> it opens up the secret heart.
> Master Paul, love's rushing flow,
> my heart awash in sacred glow.

> **O Holy Spirit, flow through me,**
> **I am the open door for thee.**
> **O mighty rushing stream of Light,**
> **transcendence is my sacred right.**

4. Serapis Bey, I consciously see that my spiritual progress does not depend on me changing any condition outside myself. It depends on one thing only, namely that I realize that no condition in the material universe can define me as a spiritual being.

> Master Paul, accelerate,
> upon pure love I meditate.
> Master Paul, intentions pure,
> my self-transcendence will ensure.

> **O Holy Spirit, flow through me,**
> **I am the open door for thee.**
> **O mighty rushing stream of Light,**
> **transcendence is my sacred right.**

9 | *Invoking Love-Based Intentions*

5. Serapis Bey, I am willing to overcome my fear of physical conditions, so that I do not have to experience those conditions. I want to overcome my fears right now, so that I can live the rest of my life without fearing any condition in the material world.

> Master Paul, your love will heal,
> my inner light you do reveal.
> Master Paul, all life console,
> with you I'm being truly whole.
>
> **O Holy Spirit, flow through me,**
> **I am the open door for thee.**
> **O mighty rushing stream of Light,**
> **transcendence is my sacred right.**

6. Serapis Bey, I consciously surrender not only the fear of the secondary laws of nature but even the desire to master those laws. I surrender all desires for deciding what Spirit should or should not do through me.

> Master Paul, you serve the All,
> by helping us transcend the fall.
> Master Paul, in peace we rise,
> as ego meets its sure demise.
>
> **O Holy Spirit, flow through me,**
> **I am the open door for thee.**
> **O mighty rushing stream of Light,**
> **transcendence is my sacred right.**

7. Serapis Bey, help me set my creativity free, so I am truly creative in seeing a higher vision and manifesting it, rather than compensating for the conditions I currently see on earth.

> Master Paul, love all life free,
> your love is for eternity.
> Master Paul, you are the One,
> to help us make the journey fun.

**O Holy Spirit, flow through me,**
**I am the open door for thee.**
**O mighty rushing stream of Light,**
**transcendence is my sacred right.**

8. Serapis Bey, I consciously surrender my reaction to the current imperfect conditions, and I surrender my desire to change them. I see that true creativity is to bring forth something that is so new that it replaces conditions that are currently here.

> Master Paul, you balance all,
> the seven rays upon my call.
> Master Paul, you paint the sky,
> with colors that delight the I.

**O Holy Spirit, flow through me,**
**I am the open door for thee.**
**O mighty rushing stream of Light,**
**transcendence is my sacred right.**

9. Serapis Bey, I consciously surrender all desire to have the fallen beings be my opponents in a dualistic game. I see that my true goal, my love-based intention, is to demonstrate that there is an alternative to the dualistic state of consciousness.

Master Paul, your Presence here,
filling up my inner sphere.
Life is now a sacred flow,
God Love I do on all bestow.

**O Holy Spirit, flow through me,
I am the open door for thee.
O mighty rushing stream of Light,
transcendence is my sacred right.**

## *Sealing:*

In the name of the Divine Mother, I fully accept that the power of these calls is used to set free the Ma-ter light, so it can outpicture the perfect vision of Christ for my own life, for all people and for the planet. In the name I AM THAT I AM, it is done! Amen.

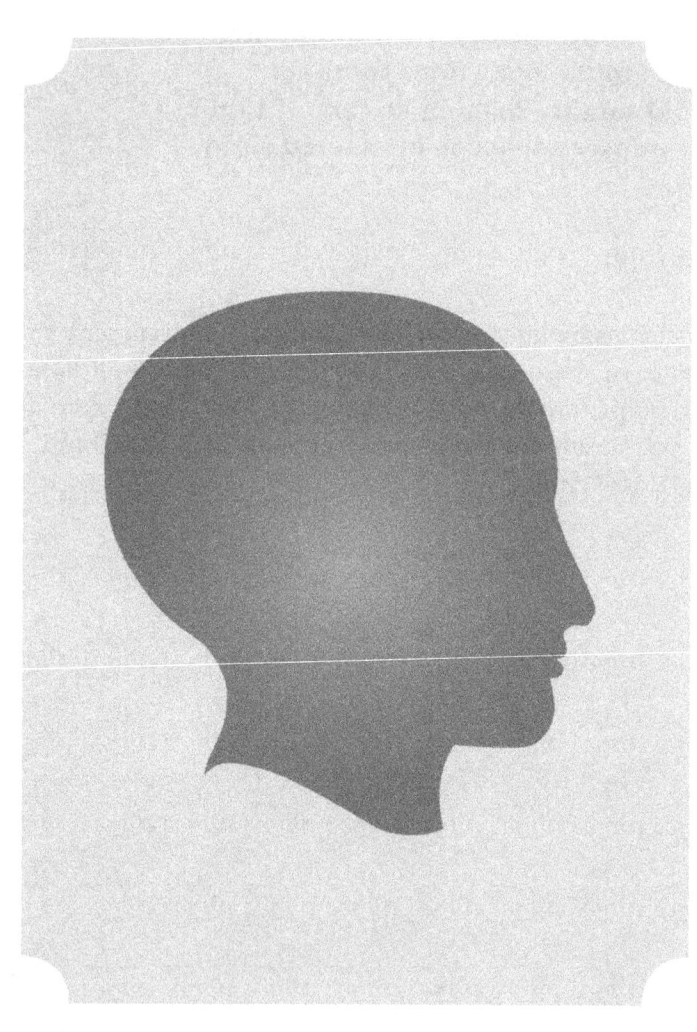

# 10 | DEVELOPING SELF-SUFFICIENT INTENTIONS

I AM the Ascended Master Serapis Bey. My purpose for this discourse is to give you some conscious hints that will help you pass the initiations on the fourth level of my retreat. This is, of course, the level where you get a double dose of purity.

What I would like to start with is to have you realize that you have now reached the point on your spiritual path – on the path of self-mastery – where you need to manifest your own built-in, inherent, self-sufficient motivation for walking the path. We of the Chohans know that we have to start people out gently. On the first three levels we give you certain teachings, certain techniques that you can respond to. It is, as I said in my last discourse, in recognition of the fact that for most people life has for so long been a tennis match where they are used to somebody sending the ball back at them, and, therefore, there is always something to react to. We need you to come to a point where your motivation for walking the spiritual path is not a reaction to or against anything in the material world.

We understand very well that this can be a difficult initiation because many of you have – whether you have been aware consciously or intuitively – been aware for a long time that there is a force that opposes your spiritual progress. You may call it the force of darkness, the force of evil, the fallen beings or whatever you may call it. It is natural that after having been aware of this for some time, you develop an idea that part of your motivation for walking the spiritual path is to get away from, to free yourself from, to cheat or to rise above the dark forces. You do understand what I am saying, do you not? It is very easy to get into the mode where your motivation for walking the spiritual path is related to – and therefore to some degree defined by – the fallen beings. I have talked about the false hierarchy, and they have been very clever in inserting many ideas that can actually distort people's view of the spiritual path to such a degree that it delays their progress or even takes them into a blind alley that it may take them lifetimes to get out of.

## Self-sufficient intentions

What I need you to do at this level of my retreat is to take an honest look at your intentions. We have said before that even fearing the false hierarchy opens you up to the false hierarchy. This may not be in the sense that the false hierarchy can directly reach into your mind and influence you that way. They *can* influence you indirectly by causing you to run away from what you fear or not be willing to look at something you fear. This causes many spiritual students to have certain elements in their own consciousness that they are not willing to look at. If you are very concerned about not following the false hierarchy, for example, you may not be willing to look at some of the ideas that they have inserted into your subconscious mind in this or past lifetimes.

You would feel so ashamed, so mortified, so terrified if you had to admit that you had certain elements of the fallen consciousness in your subconscious mind. You may even fear that I, Serapis Bey, would reject you if it was exposed that you had such elements. This, of course, will not help you take advantage of the help I offer you.

As I have already said, you cannot hide anything from me. There is hardly any person that comes to my retreat on the path of self-mastery who does not have elements of the fallen consciousness or beliefs created by the fallen beings, the false hierarchy, in their subconscious minds. How can you be alive on this planet for several lifetimes without being affected by the many illusions and lies that are out there? For me there is nothing unusual, there is nothing negative, there is nothing I need to judge about you having these elements. I am not here to judge you, shame you or find fault. I am here to help you transcend everything that limits you on the spiritual path. One of the things that will limit you is if you have certain elements inserted by the fallen beings or the dark forces. Even if you have not had anything directly inserted, you may have that fear – which in a way is also an insertion – and just seeking to avoid looking at something will, of course, hold you back on the path. It can be no other way.

I need you to come to the point where you realize that your real motivation for walking the spiritual path should not be in any way related to the dark forces or the false hierarchy. Your real motivation should come from within and should be related to your own Divine plan for this lifetime, in the short run, and in the long run to your original purpose for coming to earth. I propose that you ponder this very carefully with your conscious mind. Again, you may find it helpful to make a list of the intentions and the motives that you have that you can see are based on some kind of reaction towards the dark forces. Is there anything you are seeking to avoid, to run away from, to raise yourself above?

I need you to consciously contemplate what it is that you truly love about spirituality and about life. Many times we see students come to my retreat and they have so many limitations programmed into their minds that they dare not even really consider what they truly want. I ask you to perform an exercise where you take a piece of paper, you give the invocation based on this discourse and then afterwards you write down whatever comes to you about the topic of what you really want to do in life. I need you to be conscious of the fact that you need to set aside the limitations you have. I am asking you, in the beginning, to approach this as a theoretical exercise. You are saying that if – theoretically – you did not have any of the limitations you are facing in your current situation or in your psychology, what is it you would really like to do?

I am not asking you to speculate on what *I* want you to do, what other ascended masters want you to do or what God wants you to do. I am not asking you to speculate on what the fallen beings do *not* want you to do. I am not asking you to think about what other people do or don't want you to do. I am asking you to consider – if you had no limitations whatsoever – what would *you* really like to do in life?

## Different types of intentions

You will notice that the answers to this question may fall into two categories. There may be some that relate to unfulfilled desires and dreams that you have. Something you have never been able to do but that you have always wanted to do. There is nothing wrong with this. It may be experiences you have desired to have.

What I ask you to do is look beyond this, and then consider that there is also another category and these are things that you want to do, not so much for a personal purpose but more for an impersonal purpose. You may see this as a service to life; you may see this as a desire to change something on this planet, to bring some kind of positive change. As we have said many times, most of you who are spiritual people volunteered to come to this planet in order to bring positive change by bringing your light, your insights, your momentums and your experiences. There will be a certain percentage of the things you want to do in life that relate to this, a desire to change something on earth.

I now need you to look more closely at these. Perhaps you may give the invocation again or give my decree some times. Perhaps you may sit calmly and quietly, close your eyes and meditate upon this. What I desire you to do is to begin to see beyond all of the things that you *want* to do, that you feel *obligated* to do or that you feel you *should* do in order to make a change on earth. I need you to see that beyond these activities, there will be some motives, some intentions, that do not relate to you wanting to do anything outside yourself. Instead, they relate to what gives you the most joy in your own being.

You may not be able to see this very clearly in the beginning. You may find it difficult to put words on it. What I am seeking to help you discover here is that your original motivation for coming to earth had an Alpha and an Omega aspect. The Omega aspect was that you wanted to bring certain changes because you saw that there were conditions on this earth that needed to be left behind. The Alpha aspect was that you wanted to share your light, your I AM Presence, your God flame, your unique individual matrix. You wanted to express your individuality in a creative way. I have talked about the fact that walking the spiritual path is not a straitjacket. It still gives you room for individual creativity. This individual creativity is, in its pure form, not directed at producing certain changes that are a reaction to the way conditions currently are on earth. Creativity in its pure form is related to expressing who you are, your Divine individuality. The pure expression of creativity is not a matter of producing outer results, outer changes, especially not changes that are dependent on the choices of other beings with free will, be they in physical embodiment or the fallen beings in other realms.

Creativity in its essence is related to expressing who you are for the pure joy that it gives you to feel the light that God gave you flowing through the prism of the individuality that God gave you. I understand that you may not be able to tune in to this consciously at the moment. By pondering it and making calls about it, you will gradually begin to get some sense of this. It is very important that you get a sense of what gives you this pure sense of joy that is not related to anything outside yourself because this is the purest intention you have for being on earth. It is also an intention that you can express regardless of the outer conditions or limitations you are facing.

## Your highest motivation

I had you do the exercise of saying: "What if I didn't have any limitations? What would I express?" I now ask you to take this to a higher level where you realize that, regardless of what limitations you are facing in your outer situation, there is nothing in those limitations that can prevent you from being the open door for the light and the individuality of your I AM Presence to flow through you. This can be done in *any* situation and this is what I need you to ponder. This is the only way that you are going to develop a motivation that comes completely from inside yourself and therefore cannot be affected by, destroyed by or held back by anything outside yourself.

On the path of self-mastery there must come a point where your motivation for walking the path is only related to your conscious desire, your conscious vision, of wanting to express who you really are in the material world. This is the highest motivation for walking the path, and it is what you need in order to pass the initiations under the Chohans on the Fifth, Sixth and Seventh Ray. That is why I am the one who prepares you for those rays because you are now in the eye of the needle, the nexus.

When you begin to get a feel for your inner being and what gives you joy, you can also begin to take a look at your outer situation. I have so many students who come to me and when we sit at my retreat and take a look at their outer situation, they so often say: "But Serapis, can't you see I'm facing these limitations in my outer situation? How can I be truly spiritual, how can I express my creativity when I face these situations every day of my life? How can I quit my job, abandon my children and family and do something that is entirely creative or spiritual?"

That is not what we of the Chohans are asking you to do. There is a false motivation that has been created by the fallen beings, the false hierarchy, over many centuries. In previous centuries, it was often expressed, for example, in the Christian culture by the entire monastic culture. There was a belief that if you were a truly religious person, you would devote your life to God by going into a monastery.

You would withdraw from ordinary human life because it was considered to be in opposition to true spiritual devotion and worship of God. It was considered that God actually valued these people who withdrew from ordinary life, isolated themselves in a very comfortable environment where they were not confronted by many aspects of their own ego and therefore did not make spiritual progress or did not make significant spiritual progress.

This is not what we of the ascended masters look at as the ideal. There was a time where it was valuable for some people to be able to withdraw in order to gather momentum on the spiritual path. This does not mean that all people who lived in monasteries made progress. In today's world, in the Aquarian Age, it is, as we have said many times, not necessary or even constructive that too many people withdraw from society. It is far more important that you are spiritual and find a way to express your spirituality in everyday life. It is important that you do not isolate yourselves but demonstrate how to be spiritual even in an anti-spiritual society.

It is important for your own growth that you do not isolate yourself in spiritual communities where the members can all validate each other. They can live very comfortably without having their egos disturbed so that they are forced to see them. So many spiritual communities function this way. If people are convinced that they are spiritual, but they are all validating each others egos, they are not helping each other see the ego and thus they are not overcoming them.

## *Seeing Serapis as a facilitator not a teacher*

I need you to realize that it is, for the vast majority of the spiritual people in this age, necessary, constructive and in accordance with your Divine plan to find a way to express your spirituality and your creativity regardless of the outer circumstances you are facing. In order for this to be successful, you need to make a shift in your consciousness.

The first shift you need to make is that you do not look at me as a traditional teacher. So far, I and the three first Chohans that you have encountered have acted to some degree as the teachers you found on earth. We have been the ones who have taken the initiative in our retreats. We have presented you with certain lessons, exercises and challenges and you have responded to them. You may, of course, have had a motivation that caused you to enter our retreats and to engage in the path of self-mastery. Once you are in our retreats, it has often been so that in your conscious minds your primary motivation has been related to us and following the initiations, passing the initiations, not disappointing us or whatever you have felt. I need you to make a switch where your motivation for being in my retreat and for interacting with me is not based on wanting to please me, to follow me or, for that matter, to oppose me. I need you to make the switch where you realize that you are in my retreat because you want to overcome whatever obstacles are preventing you from being the open door for the creative expression of the light and individuality that you truly are and that is anchored in your I AM Presence.

I need you to make a switch to a love-based motivation for being here. I am quite capable of feeling when students have a reaction to me. They either have a desire to please me or they have a certain obstruction in their consciousness so that they are reluctantly following my instructions. This is what you need to overcome at the fourth level of my retreat. I need you to come to a point where, regardless of how you have looked at me or ascended masters in the past, you can now relate to me in a completely open and neutral way. I am not your disciplinarian, I am not the one who looks down at you, I am not the one who exposes or shames you. I am not the one who makes demands on you.

I am here to facilitate your growth but I am not the motivation. *You* need to supply the motivation entirely from within. There actually comes a point at the fourth level where I gather the students who are ready and we go into a room. Before we go in, I tell them that the purpose is that they will receive their primary motivation for walking the path from this point forward. I, of course, say this in such a way that the students in most cases believe that I will give them this motivation. Then we enter the room, we sit down and then I simply sit there and I look from student to student. I look those in the eyes who are willing to look me in the eye, but I say nothing.

It takes a while before the students start looking at me with these big question marks in their eyes. It takes an even longer while before some of them begin to ask: "So Serapis, when are you going to give us our motive?" I still sit there and look and smile, and then there is usually one or two in the group that suddenly look at the others and say: "Maybe he really means that we need to get it from within?" Then, usually, the light is turned on in the eyes of most of the students.

Some may not be willing to do this. In some cases a student has had to leave and go back and take other initiations. In most cases the students now become very eager and then they close their eyes and go within. What I can do for them at this point is, of course, that because they are in my aura, I can shield them from all of the impure motives that normally pull on their minds. In my Presence, they have a greater opportunity to discover what I have talked about that gives them the greatest joy.

## Being an equal with Serapis

After the students discover at least some of their inner motivation, there is always a shift. Suddenly, there is none of the wanting to please me or the reluctance or other artificial elements in their attitude and relationship to me. We can now begin to interact in an entirely different way. The students are not waiting for me to do something and take the initiative, instead *they* take the initiative, *they* come and ask me: "Serapis, I would like to see this, I would like to understand this, I would like to develop this ability, what do you think about this?" All of a sudden, we are acting not as teacher and student but as equals.

I am not above the students, I am not above you. I just have more experience and perhaps more vision. Instead of being the high and mighty teacher that is standing at the head of the class, looking down upon the students, I am now what I always wanted to be: the facilitator. At this point, we go through various exercises, and I tell you this because it is important for your own growth at this level that you also go through some of these exercises with your conscious mind.

What I need you to realize at this level is that there are two elements of your growth, the Alpha and the Omega. The Alpha is, of course, that you get to the point where you express your creativity from within, from your I AM Presence. The Omega is that in order to get to that point, there are certain things you need to see in your own consciousness. In order to see those things, you often need to experience certain situations in the material world.

## The belief that things are not spiritual

This means that you can make another very important shift in your attitude to the material world, to the Mother realm, in the way you look at the world. One of the very subtle hooks created by the false hierarchy over a long period of time is the idea that there are certain things in the world that are not spiritual, that are not pure and that will not facilitate your spiritual growth.

We have said before that all the fallen beings had to do to really mess up things on earth was to create the idea that:

- There is a standard

- Everything must be judged according to the standard.

The fallen beings have created the standard that something is spiritual and something is not spiritual. Then, they have projected that if you are a religious or spiritual person, you need to evaluate everything on earth based on this standard. You now have many spiritual people who are using a considerable amount of energy and attention on evaluating everything they do, everything they encounter, in the material world. They do not do this in a neutral way; they do it based on a value judgment of what is spiritual and what is not spiritual. The underlying belief or assumption is, of course, that something which is labeled as not spiritual will oppose your growth. This is precisely what the false hierarchy wants you to believe.

You do understand, do you not, that you are no longer below the 48th level of consciousness? Otherwise, you would not be at this fourth level in my retreat. There are people below the 48th level who need to have the evaluation that certain things are not spiritual. Surely, you cannot make progress on the spiritual path if you are running around killing other people, stealing from them or engaged in other forms of criminal activity. There are people who need to have a certain standard, saying: "This is not spiritual, this will prevent me from going to heaven or prevent me from making progress on the spiritual path." I am not talking about these people.

I am talking about *you* who are at the fourth level of the Fourth Ray on the path of self-mastery. I need you, right now, to take another look at your standards for evaluating what is spiritual and non-spiritual. My goal for this is to get you to a point where you realize that, regardless of what conditions you are facing right now, you can still be spiritual and you can still express your God-given creativity and individuality.

I need you to transcend another subtle hook of the false hierarchy, which is that when certain outer conditions are fulfilled, *then* you can truly be spiritual. This is the illusion you need to overcome, and you do this by realizing that the evaluation or the judgment which says that this condition or this activity is spiritual and that condition or that activity is not spiritual, is not the highest way to look at things.

You will not make progress beyond this point by thinking that there are certain activities that are not spiritual and that you must avoid, and there are other activities that are spiritual and you must seek them out. What I need you to realize is that, right now, your progress on the path depends on you seeing certain conditions, certain patterns, certain matrices in your four lower bodies that are limiting the expression of your creativity, your creative powers.

In order to see these, you need to have certain experiences in the material world. The conditions you are facing right now are not an enemy of your spiritual growth. You need to not look at them based on the simplistic evaluation, the black-and-white evaluation, the dualistic evaluation of whether they are spiritual or anti-spiritual. You need to look at them and realize that these conditions are an expression of a certain state of consciousness. They give you an opportunity to see something about yourself based on how you react to these conditions.

You may be facing a certain situation where there are some things that you, from a superficial black-and-white evaluation, would say these are not spiritual, these are not pure. You may so far have been trying to avoid them, to deny them, to reject them, to get away from them. What I need you to do is make the shift and say: "What are these conditions meant to teach me about myself? How am I reacting to these conditions? What does my reaction say about what I feel, what I believe or how I see myself in relation to the material world?"

## The Alpha and Omega of identity

What you have in your identity body is an Alpha and an Omega aspect. The Alpha aspect is in your higher identity body, and it is a view from below of the individuality in your I AM Presence. Many people cannot see this consciously because it is obscured by the Omega aspect of your sense of identity. This is the sense of identity you have built over your many lifetimes of embodiment on earth.

This sense of identity is how you see yourself in relation to the material world, to the Mother realm. It is this identity you need to uncover, question, see for the unreality that it is and gradually transcend. It is this identity that makes you believe that because you are in a physical body, because you are in this or that situation, you cannot express your true individuality and your true creativity. Surely, you have certain patterns in your emotional body, certain beliefs in your mental body, that also block your creativity. They are at a lower level than the sense of identity of what you can or cannot do, what you are allowed or not allowed to do in this world. I need you to ponder this with your conscious mind whereby you will make the maximum use of the lessons you receive at my retreat at night.

It has been said that to the pure everything is pure, and truly there is some reality there. I would rather go one step further and say that to the person who is pure in consciousness, the evaluation of whether something is pure or impure simply falls away. You are not looking at your life, your conditions, and saying: "Oh, this is impure; I want to avoid it." Instead, you are saying: "There must be a reason why this condition has manifested itself in my life, there must be something I am meant to learn from it."

This does not mean that you embrace the *condition,* but it means that you embrace the *lesson.* Instead of running away from the condition, and thereby running away from the lesson, you *embrace* the lesson. There are many spiritual people who, in order to overcome a certain limitation in their psychology, have to take certain steps, have to go through certain experiences that may, from the black-and-white perspective, seem to be anti-spiritual or impure. Many of you will be able to look at your lives and see that you have gone through certain situations that have been either impure, not spiritual, hurtful or that you now feel very embarrassed about.

## *The cause of humiliation*

You were very humiliated by those conditions, but you can, if you are willing to make the shift I am talking about, overcome these feelings and realize that you had to go through these conditions in order to overcome something in yourself. There may be a lesson you had to learn about a certain belief about what you can or cannot do in this world. It may be that you simply had to be humiliated in order to overcome a certain sense of pride.

Many spiritual people have a considerable momentum on doing well in the material world. For example, there are many people who in a past life have been privileged, belonging to a privileged elite. You have been rich, you have been born into a rich and powerful family, you have had a certain position and privilege in society that meant you did not have to experience some of the conditions that so-called ordinary people go through.

You may therefore have come to see it as being very humiliating to experience such conditions, but why did you feel that way? You felt that way because you had built a certain pride that you were somehow better than others because you had a privileged position. This is not to say that most spiritual people are fallen beings, but it is a fact that many of the more mature spiritual people have embodied in families with fallen beings, both so that the spiritual people could learn something and so that the fallen beings could have an opportunity to see an alternative approach to life. It is very easy to take on this subtle belief of the fallen beings that, because you have a privileged position in society, you are better than other people and therefore there are certain things that you should not be exposed to.

If you *are* exposed to these conditions, you will feel humiliated. If this is the case, I ask you to consider whether it was not the entire purpose that you had a chance to overcome your sense of pride, to simply leave it behind. There is another possibility for why you have experienced certain limiting or humiliating conditions. It may be that you have to see a pattern in your psychology, it may be that you have to overcome pride or it may also be that you wanted to bring yourself to a point where you manifested the willpower that you have not manifested in past lives.

## Manifesting a higher will power

When I say that you have to have a certain experience until you have had enough of it, this can have various aspects. There are certain experiences that relate to the body that can give you a sense of pleasure. Most people find that they have, over several lifetimes, had to have such experiences to a certain extent before they begin to feel saturated and are no longer so attached to these bodily desires. There is a higher level of this, and it is that there are certain conditions you experience for the purpose of bringing you to the point where you make a conscious decision of saying: "This is enough, I do not want to experience this anymore."

This messenger himself has had the experience within recent years of coming to the realization that he had a mistaken belief that it was his role to try to help everybody who claimed to be interested in walking the spiritual path, even people who were fallen beings or who had a very negative view of life or themselves. He then came to the realization that the reason he had attracted such people to him was that he needed to manifest the willpower to say: "No more, I do not want these kinds of people in my life." You may face a similar initiation in another outer disguise and clothing. It is important to contemplate that there may be certain conditions in your life that you are attracting to you over and over again for the one and only reason that you have not made a firm decision that you no longer want to deal with this condition.

It may be necessary, of course, to then look at yourself and say: "What is the belief I have that attracts this condition to me and makes me feel like I am obligated, I have to have it or I have to respond to it?" In the example of this messenger, he realized that he believed that he had to be able to help everybody. Well, this is in a sense a form of pride because none of us can help everybody. There is no spiritual teacher – there never has been, there never will be – who could help all people in embodiment. There will be some that you simply cannot reach no matter who you are. This messenger thought that if there were people he could not help, it was because there was something wrong with him. *He* was not good enough, he did not know enough, he had not developed certain abilities. He constantly thought he had to change himself in order to accommodate other people.

## Changing yourself to accommodate others

This is another subtle hook of the fallen beings that they insert into the minds of almost everyone in various disguises. They make you think that because you are on the spiritual path and you are willing to change yourself, here is a condition where you need to change yourself in relation to that condition. You need to tie knots on yourself in order to accommodate these other kinds of people, in order to be able help them or do something in the material world.

In many cases, the initiation is that you must come to the point of saying: "But I don't want to do this. This is not in accordance with my higher desire for what I want to express on earth. I do not want to deal with these kinds of people. I do not want to change myself in order to accommodate these people who are not willing to walk the path, who are not willing to look at themselves. They are seeking to change me in order to avoid changing themselves, and I am not willing to

## 10 | Developing Self-Sufficient Intentions

go along with this anymore. I am not willing to change myself in order to accommodate those who are not willing to change themselves. I will change myself, and I will change myself right now by making the conscious decision that I do not want these people in my life. I am replacing the belief that I should change myself in order to accommodate them with the realization that I have a right to be who I am and express my God-given individuality, regardless of what these people think about it."

It is an eternal fact that spiritual students can be divided into roughly two categories. There are those who are very sure of themselves and who often have a certain pride and a certain feeling that they know better than the teacher how the teacher should teach them. These students it is very hard for a spiritual teacher to help.

Then, there is the other kind of students who are very humble, who are very open to the teacher's directions and who are very open to changing themselves. They are teachable but only up to a point. There comes a point where you cannot make progress by following the teacher, you have to start making your own decisions. You have to decide what you want and do not want in your life.

## Everything is spiritual

It might help you to look at your life, to look at the way you evaluate what is spiritual and unspiritual, and realize that when your true goal is to grow, there is really nothing on earth that is impure or not spiritual. If you need to have a certain experience in order to see something about yourself, then having that experience is not anti-spiritual.

I also need you to take a look at this standard for what is spiritual and realize that the false hierarchy has used it to get many people to focus their attention on avoiding something. Let us take an obvious example: sexuality. So many spiritual people have various beliefs about sex not being spiritual, certain forms of sex not being spiritual or certain sexual activities not being spiritual.

You have the old monastic culture where you had to totally avoid sex. You even have it in the Catholic Church of forbidding priests to be married. I am not concerned about whether you have sex or not. I am concerned about whether sex takes up attention that could be used for spiritual growth. Do you see what I am saying?

If you think sex is impure and you force yourself to avoid it, you are creating a strain in your mind that distracts you from spiritual growth. If you think sex is impure or certain forms of sex are impure and you are constantly evaluating but still having sex, then you are again tying up your attention.

What I need you to realize is that, whether it is sex or other physical activities, the activity in itself is not impure. What you need to do is come to a point where you simply make a decision. I have no problem with a student saying: "I desire to experience sex" and then you experience it in a responsible way that does not hurt yourself and others. Then, you don't let it occupy your attention.

It is something you do and it doesn't pull on your attention. It doesn't cause you constant emotional turmoil, constant arguing with yourself whether this is okay or not. It doesn't make you feel that: "Oh, am I really a spiritual person because I'm doing this or should I not be doing it?" I need you to get to the point where there is no tension related to the physical activities you engage in. You engage in it, you appreciate and enjoy the experience and then you focus most of your attention on other things.

## 10 | Developing Self-Sufficient Intentions

I have given you a considerable mouthful, but that is because the fourth level of my retreat is another one of these where you really cannot move beyond until you have had certain breakthroughs. I know we recommend that you give each lesson or each invocation once a day for nine days. It may be very constructive for you to give the invocation for the fourth level for more than nine days, to read this discourse over and over again, to ponder what I have said, to make your lists or to at least meditate on the conditions and the hints I have given you.

I would like you to not set a time limit for how long you are going to work on this lesson. Keep doing it until you honestly feel: "Now, I am ready to move on." I am not telling you how long that should be. It could be one day, it could be nine, it could be more. I am just asking you to tune in to when you feel from within that you are ready. I am *not* asking you to decide with your outer mind. I am, in fact, asking you to be conscious of whether your outer mind wants you to complete the lesson quickly out of pride or wants you to draw it out, out of a false pride, a false humility. Work on this lesson until you know from within: "Now I am ready," then move on to the fifth level of initiation,

Serapis Bey I AM.

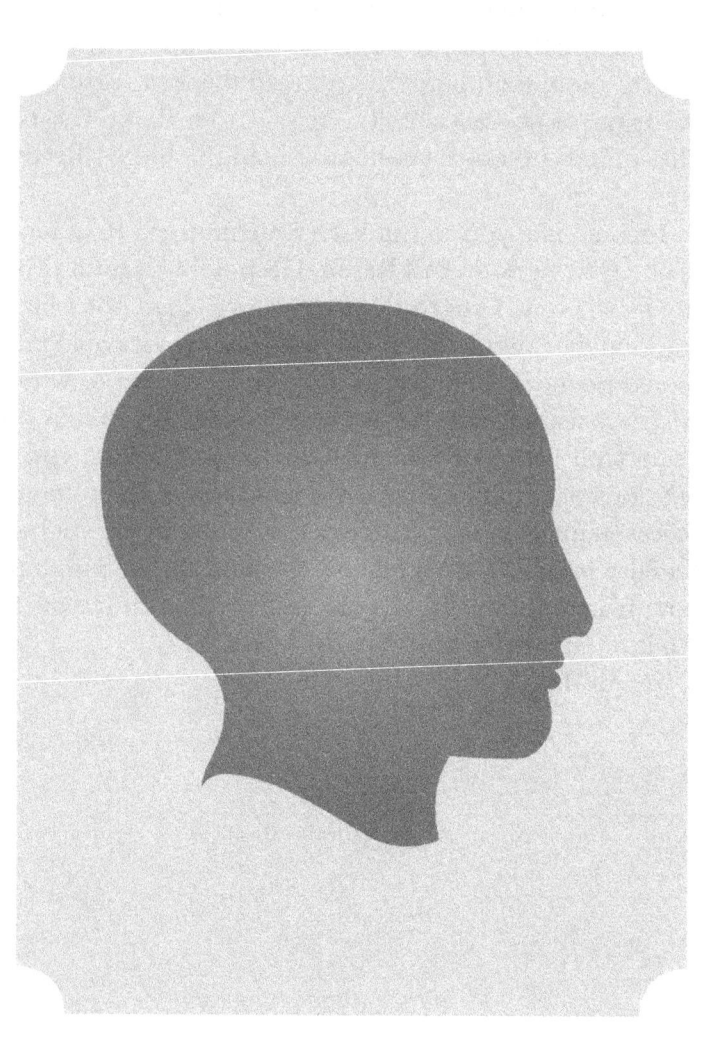

# 11 | INVOKING SELF-SUFFICIENT INTENTIONS

In the name I AM THAT I AM, Jesus Christ, I call to my I AM Presence to flow through the I Will Be Presence that I AM and give this invocation with full power. I call to beloved Elohim Purity and Astrea, Archangel Gabriel and Hope and Serapis Bey to help me transcend all lesser intentions and discover my inner intention for being in embodiment. Help me see and surrender all patterns that block my oneness with Serapis Bey and with my I AM Presence, including …

[Make personal calls]

*Part 1*

1. Serapis Bey, I am manifesting my own built-in, inherent and self-sufficient motivation for walking the path. I consciously surrender all motives for getting away from, freeing myself from, cheating or rising above the dark forces.

Beloved Astrea, your heart is so true,
your Circle and Sword of white and blue,
cut all life free from dramas unwise,
on wings of Purity our planet will rise.

**Beloved Astrea, in God Purity,**
**accelerate all of my life energy,**
**raising my mind into true unity**
**with the Masters of love in Infinity.**

2. Serapis Bey, I consciously surrender all motives for walking the spiritual path that are related to – and therefore defined by – the fallen beings, the false hierarchy.

Beloved Astrea, from Purity's Ray,
send forth deliverance to all life today,
acceleration to Purity, I AM now free
from all that is less than love's Purity.

**Beloved Astrea, in oneness with you,**
**your circle and sword of electric blue,**
**with Purity's Light cutting right through,**
**raising within me all that is true.**

3. Serapis Bey, I consciously surrender all fear of the false hierarchy. I surrender all fear that you would reject me if it was exposed that I had elements of the fallen consciousness. I am willing to take advantage of the help you offer me.

Beloved Astrea, accelerate us all,
as for your deliverance I fervently call,
set all life free from vision impure
beyond fear and doubt, I AM rising for sure.

## 11 | Invoking Self-Sufficient Intentions

**Beloved Astrea, I AM willing to see,
all of the lies that keep me unfree,
I AM rising beyond every impurity,
with Purity's Light forever in me.**

4. Serapis Bey, I consciously surrender all illusions saying that I am already free from the fallen consciousness. Help me transcend all elements inserted by the fallen beings or the dark forces.

Beloved Astrea, accelerate life
beyond all duality's struggle and strife,
consume all division between God and man,
accelerate fulfillment of God's perfect plan.

**Beloved Astrea, I lovingly call,
break down separation's invisible wall,
I surrender all lies causing the fall,
forever affirming the oneness of All.**

5. Serapis Bey, help me see any intentions and motives that are based on a reaction to the dark forces. Help me see anything I am seeking to avoid, to run away from, to raise myself above.

Beloved Astrea, your heart is so true,
your Circle and Sword of white and blue,
cut all life free from dramas unwise,
on wings of Purity our planet will rise.

**Beloved Astrea, in God Purity,
accelerate all of my life energy,
raising my mind into true unity
with the Masters of love in Infinity.**

6. Serapis Bey, help me see what I truly love. Help me see beyond all of the things that I want to do, that I feel obligated to do or that I feel I should do in order to make a change on earth. Help me see the intentions that relate to what gives me the most joy in my own being.

> Beloved Astrea, from Purity's Ray,
> send forth deliverance to all life today,
> acceleration to Purity, I AM now free
> from all that is less than love's Purity.
>
> **Beloved Astrea, in oneness with you,**
> **your circle and sword of electric blue,**
> **with Purity's Light cutting right through,**
> **raising within me all that is true.**

7. Serapis Bey, help me see what I wanted to share in terms of my light, my I AM Presence, my God flame, my unique individual matrix. Help me see how to express my individuality in a creative way.

> Beloved Astrea, accelerate us all,
> as for your deliverance I fervently call,
> set all life free from vision impure
> beyond fear and doubt, I AM rising for sure.
>
> **Beloved Astrea, I AM willing to see,**
> **all of the lies that keep me unfree,**
> **I AM rising beyond every impurity,**
> **with Purity's Light forever in me.**

8. Serapis Bey, help me see my individual creativity in its pure form as it is related to expressing who I am, my Divine individuality. Help me feel the pure joy of having the light of God flowing through the prism of the individuality that God gave me.

> Beloved Astrea, accelerate life
> beyond all duality's struggle and strife,
> consume all division between God and man,
> accelerate fulfillment of God's perfect plan.
>
> **Beloved Astrea, I lovingly call,**
> **break down separation's invisible wall,**
> **I surrender all lies causing the fall,**
> **forever affirming the oneness of All.**

9. Serapis Bey, I see that what gives me this pure sense of joy, that is not related to anything outside myself, is also an intention that I can express regardless of the outer conditions or limitations I am facing.

> Accelerate into Purity, I AM real,
> Accelerate into Purity, all life heal,
> Accelerate into Purity, I AM MORE,
> Accelerate into Purity, all will soar.

Accelerate into Purity! (3X)
Beloved Elohim Astrea.
Accelerate into Purity! (3X)
Beloved Gabriel and Hope.
Accelerate into Purity! (3X)
Beloved Serapis Bey.
Accelerate into Purity! (3X)
Beloved I AM.

## Part 2

1. Serapis Bey, I see that, regardless of what limitations I am facing in my outer situation, there is nothing in those limitations that can prevent me from being the open door for the light and the individuality of my I AM Presence.

> Gabriel Archangel, your light I revere,
> immersed in your Presence, nothing I fear.
> A disciple of Christ, I do leave behind,
> the ego's desire for responding in kind.
>
> **Gabriel Archangel, of this I am sure,**
> **Gabriel Archangel, Christ light is the cure.**
> **Gabriel Archangel, intentions so pure,**
> **Gabriel Archangel, in you I'm secure.**

2. Serapis Bey, I consciously affirm that my motivation for walking the path is only related to my conscious desire, my conscious vision, of wanting to express who I really am in the material world.

## 11 | Invoking Self-Sufficient Intentions

> Gabriel Archangel, I fear not the light,
> in purifications' fire, I delight.
> With your hand in mine, each challenge I face,
> I follow the spiral to infinite grace.
>
> **Gabriel Archangel, of this I am sure,**
> **Gabriel Archangel, Christ light is the cure.**
> **Gabriel Archangel, intentions so pure,**
> **Gabriel Archangel, in you I'm secure.**

3. Serapis Bey, I consciously surrender all desire to withdraw from ordinary human life and isolate myself in a very comfortable environment where I am not confronted by many aspects of my own ego.

> Gabriel Archangel, your fire burning white,
> ascending with you, out of the night.
> My ego has nowhere to run and to hide,
> in ascension's bright spiral, with you I abide.
>
> **Gabriel Archangel, of this I am sure,**
> **Gabriel Archangel, Christ light is the cure.**
> **Gabriel Archangel, intentions so pure,**
> **Gabriel Archangel, in you I'm secure.**

4. Serapis Bey, help me find a way to be spiritual and to express my spirituality in everyday life. I am willing to demonstrate how to be spiritual in an anti-spiritual society.

> Gabriel Archangel, your trumpet I hear,
> announcing the birth of Christ drawing near.
> In lightness of being, I now am reborn,
> rising with Christ on bright Easter morn.

**Gabriel Archangel, of this I am sure,
Gabriel Archangel, Christ light is the cure.
Gabriel Archangel, intentions so pure,
Gabriel Archangel, in you I'm secure.**

5. Serapis Bey, help me make a shift in consciousness so I see the way to express my spirituality and my creativity regardless of the outer circumstances I am facing.

> Gabriel Archangel, your light I revere,
> immersed in your Presence, nothing I fear.
> A disciple of Christ, I do leave behind,
> the ego's desire for responding in kind.

**Gabriel Archangel, of this I am sure,
Gabriel Archangel, Christ light is the cure.
Gabriel Archangel, intentions so pure,
Gabriel Archangel, in you I'm secure.**

6. Serapis Bey, I consciously surrender all desire to please you, to follow you or to oppose you. I want to overcome whatever obstacles are preventing me from being the open door for the creative expression of the light and individuality that is anchored in my I AM Presence.

> Gabriel Archangel, I fear not the light,
> in purifications' fire, I delight.
> With your hand in mine, each challenge I face,
> I follow the spiral to infinite grace.

## 11 | Invoking Self-Sufficient Intentions

> Gabriel Archangel, of this I am sure,
> Gabriel Archangel, Christ light is the cure.
> Gabriel Archangel, intentions so pure,
> Gabriel Archangel, in you I'm secure.

7. Serapis Bey, I am willing to supply the motivation entirely from within. I am willing to interact with you, not as teacher and student but as equals.

Gabriel Archangel, your fire burning white,
ascending with you, out of the night.
My ego has nowhere to run and to hide,
in ascension's bright spiral, with you I abide.

> Gabriel Archangel, of this I am sure,
> Gabriel Archangel, Christ light is the cure.
> Gabriel Archangel, intentions so pure,
> Gabriel Archangel, in you I'm secure.

8. Serapis Bey, I realize that in order to be an open door for my I AM Presence, there are certain things I need to see in my own consciousness. In order to see those things, I often need to experience certain situations in the material world.

Gabriel Archangel, your trumpet I hear,
announcing the birth of Christ drawing near.
In lightness of being, I now am reborn,
rising with Christ on bright Easter morn.

> Gabriel Archangel, of this I am sure,
> Gabriel Archangel, Christ light is the cure.
> Gabriel Archangel, intentions so pure,
> Gabriel Archangel, in you I'm secure.

9. Serapis Bey, I consciously surrender the lie of the fallen beings that there are certain things in the world that are not spiritual, that are not pure and that will not facilitate my spiritual growth. I surrender the illusion that I need to judge everything according to the standard defined by the fallen beings.

> With angels I soar,
> as I reach for MORE.
> The angels so real,
> their love all will heal.
> The angels bring peace,
> all conflicts will cease.
> With angels of light,
> we soar to new height.

> **The rustling sound of angel wings,**
> **what joy as even matter sings,**
> **what joy as every atom rings,**
> **in harmony with angel wings.**

## Part 3

1. Serapis Bey, I consciously surrender the tendency to use energy and attention on evaluating everything I do, everything I encounter, in the material world. Help me see life in a neutral way that is not based on a value judgment of what is spiritual and what is not spiritual.

> Serapis Bey, what power lies,
> behind your purifying eyes.
> Serapis Bey, it is a treat,
> to enter your sublime retreat.

> **O Holy Spirit, flow through me,**
> **I am the open door for thee.**
> **O mighty rushing stream of Light,**
> **transcendence is my sacred right.**

2. Serapis Bey, show me my standards for evaluating what is spiritual and non-spiritual. I see that, regardless of what conditions I am facing right now, I can still be spiritual and express my God-given creativity and individuality.

> Serapis Bey, what wisdom found,
> your words are always most profound.
> Serapis Bey, I tell you true,
> my mind has room for naught but you.

> **O Holy Spirit, flow through me,**
> **I am the open door for thee.**
> **O mighty rushing stream of Light,**
> **transcendence is my sacred right.**

3. Serapis Bey, I consciously surrender the dream that when certain outer conditions are fulfilled, then I can truly be spiritual. I surrender the lie that there are certain activities that are not spiritual and that I must avoid, and there are other activities that are spiritual and I must seek them out.

> Serapis Bey, what love beyond,
> my heart does leap, as I respond.
> Serapis Bey, your life a poem,
> that calls me to my starry home.

**O Holy Spirit, flow through me,
I am the open door for thee.
O mighty rushing stream of Light,
transcendence is my sacred right.**

4. Serapis Bey, I see that my progress on the path depends on me seeing the conditions, patterns and matrices in my four lower bodies that are limiting the expression of my creative powers. In order to see these, I need to have certain experiences in the material world.

Serapis Bey, your guidance sure,
my base is clear and white and pure.
Serapis Bey, no longer trapped,
by soul in which my self was wrapped.

**O Holy Spirit, flow through me,
I am the open door for thee.
O mighty rushing stream of Light,
transcendence is my sacred right.**

5. Serapis Bey, I consciously see that the conditions I am facing right now are not an enemy of my spiritual growth. My conditions are an expression of a certain state of consciousness. They give me an opportunity to see something about myself based on how I react to these conditions.

Serapis Bey, what healing balm,
in mind that is forever calm.
Serapis Bey, my thoughts are pure,
your discipline I shall endure.

**O Holy Spirit, flow through me,
I am the open door for thee.
O mighty rushing stream of Light,
transcendence is my sacred right.**

6. Serapis Bey, I consciously surrender the tendency to deny conditions that I think are not spiritual. Instead, I consider what these conditions are meant to teach me about myself and what my reaction says about how I see myself in relation to the material world.

Serapis Bey, what secret test,
for egos who want to be best.
Serapis Bey, expose in me,
all that is less than harmony.

**O Holy Spirit, flow through me,
I am the open door for thee.
O mighty rushing stream of Light,
transcendence is my sacred right.**

7. Serapis Bey, help me see and transcend the Omega aspect of my sense of identity, the sense of identity I have built over many lifetimes of embodiment on earth and that determines how I see myself in relation to the material world.

Serapis Bey, what moving sight,
my self ascends to sacred height.
Serapis Bey, forever free,
in sacred synchronicity.

**O Holy Spirit, flow through me,
I am the open door for thee.
O mighty rushing stream of Light,
transcendence is my sacred right.**

8. Serapis Bey, I see that the reason a condition has manifested itself in my life is that there is something I need to learn from it. Instead of running away from the condition and thereby running away from the lesson, I embrace the lesson.

Serapis Bey, you balance all,
the seven rays upon my call.
Serapis Bey, in space and time,
the pyramid of self, I climb.

**O Holy Spirit, flow through me,
I am the open door for thee.
O mighty rushing stream of Light,
transcendence is my sacred right.**

9. Serapis Bey, I see that in order to overcome a certain limitation in my psychology, I have to take certain steps and go through certain experiences that seem anti-spiritual or impure. I see that I have gone through certain situations that I feel very embarrassed about.

Serapis Bey, your Presence here,
filling up my inner sphere.
Life is now a sacred flow,
God Purity I do bestow.

# 11 | Invoking Self-Sufficient Intentions

> **O Holy Spirit, flow through me,**
> **I am the open door for thee.**
> **O mighty rushing stream of Light,**
> **transcendence is my sacred right.**

## Part 4

1. Serapis Bey, help me make the shift and overcome these feelings. Help me accept that I had to go through these conditions in order to overcome something in myself. Help me learn the lesson from my most embarrassing experiences and transcend the sense of embarrassment.

> Serapis Bey, what power lies,
> behind your purifying eyes.
> Serapis Bey, it is a treat,
> to enter your sublime retreat.

> **O Holy Spirit, flow through me,**
> **I am the open door for thee.**
> **O mighty rushing stream of Light,**
> **transcendence is my sacred right.**

2. Serapis Bey, I consciously surrender all sense that I should have a certain position and privilege in society, and that I should not have to experience some of the conditions that so-called ordinary people go through. Help me see any element of the pride of the fallen beings and to leave it behind.

Serapis Bey, what wisdom found,
your words are always most profound.
Serapis Bey, I tell you true,
my mind has room for naught but you.

**O Holy Spirit, flow through me,
I am the open door for thee.
O mighty rushing stream of Light,
transcendence is my sacred right.**

3. Serapis Bey, help me see the experiences in my life where I need to manifest the conscious willpower and decide that I have had enough of this type of experience.

Serapis Bey, what love beyond,
my heart does leap, as I respond.
Serapis Bey, your life a poem,
that calls me to my starry home.

**O Holy Spirit, flow through me,
I am the open door for thee.
O mighty rushing stream of Light,
transcendence is my sacred right.**

4. Serapis Bey, help me see the belief I have that attracts such conditions to me and makes me feel like I have to respond a certain way. Help me see the fallen lie that says that because I am on the spiritual path and willing to change myself, I need to tie knots on myself in order to accommodate other people.

Serapis Bey, your guidance sure,
my base is clear and white and pure.
Serapis Bey, no longer trapped,
by soul in which my self was wrapped.

**O Holy Spirit, flow through me,
I am the open door for thee.
O mighty rushing stream of Light,
transcendence is my sacred right.**

5. Serapis Bey, help me see where I need to decide that I don't want to do certain things because they are not in accordance with my higher desire for what I want to express on earth. I do not want to deal with certain people. I do not want to change myself in order to accommodate these people.

Serapis Bey, what healing balm,
in mind that is forever calm.
Serapis Bey, my thoughts are pure,
your discipline I shall endure.

**O Holy Spirit, flow through me,
I am the open door for thee.
O mighty rushing stream of Light,
transcendence is my sacred right.**

6. Serapis Bey, I am making the conscious decision that I do not want certain people in my life. I am replacing the belief that I should change myself in order to accommodate them with the realization that I have a right to be who I am and express my God-given individuality, regardless of what these people think about it.

Serapis Bey, what secret test,
for egos who want to be best.
Serapis Bey, expose in me,
all that is less than harmony.

**O Holy Spirit, flow through me,
I am the open door for thee.
O mighty rushing stream of Light,
transcendence is my sacred right.**

7. Serapis Bey, help me look at my life, look at the way I evaluate what is spiritual and unspiritual, and realize that when my true goal is to grow, there is nothing on earth that is impure or not spiritual. If I need to have a certain experience in order to see something about myself, then having that experience is not anti-spiritual.

Serapis Bey, what moving sight,
my self ascends to sacred height.
Serapis Bey, forever free,
in sacred synchronicity.

**O Holy Spirit, flow through me,
I am the open door for thee.
O mighty rushing stream of Light,
transcendence is my sacred right.**

8. Serapis Bey, help me evaluate my life and transcend the tendency to let certain activities pull on my attention and take my focus away from spiritual growth. Help me accept that engaging in certain activities with pure intentions is inconsequential to my spiritual growth.

Serapis Bey, you balance all,
the seven rays upon my call.
Serapis Bey, in space and time,
the pyramid of self, I climb.

**O Holy Spirit, flow through me,
I am the open door for thee.
O mighty rushing stream of Light,
transcendence is my sacred right.**

9. Serapis Bey, I am willing to see any aspect in my consciousness and life that prevents me from passing the initiations on the fourth level of your retreat. I am truly willing to overcome these limitations and move on to the next level.

Serapis Bey, your Presence here,
filling up my inner sphere.
Life is now a sacred flow,
God Purity I do bestow.

**O Holy Spirit, flow through me,
I am the open door for thee.
O mighty rushing stream of Light,
transcendence is my sacred right.**

## Sealing:

In the name of the Divine Mother, I fully accept that the power of these calls is used to set free the Ma-ter light, so it can outpicture the perfect vision of Christ for my own life, for all people and for the planet. In the name I AM THAT I AM, it is done! Amen.

# 12 | SEEING OPPORTUNITIES FOR SELF-TRANSCENDENCE

I am the Ascended Master Serapis Bey. We have now turned an important corner in the progression of this book and the course you are taking under me as the Chohan of the Fourth Ray. As I said in my last discourse, you have now come to a point where you have a greater acceptance of me as a facilitator. You are running on your own inner motivation for walking the path. I do not need to present you anything that you can react to or react against. We need to go with your own motivation, and I simply facilitate your own discovery of what takes you higher on the path.

We have now come to the level where you face the combination of the Fourth Ray of Purity with the Fifth Ray, which has often been called the ray of vision or the ray of healing. These two are, naturally, linked. Why do you need to be healed? Because you are unwhole. Why are you unwhole? Well, because you have a distorted or limited vision, you do not have a whole vision. Naturally, purifying your vision is a key to healing as it is a key to growth. The Fifth Ray, of course, is also the ray of manifestation, materialization, using your vision to produce changes in the material world.

When you come to this point and you have the desire to purify your vision, then I will take you through a series of steps in your finer bodies. What I will do in this discourse is to take you through a series of steps in your conscious mind that can help you tune in to and also pass the initiations in my retreat. You can thereby pass the initiations consciously and anchor the lessons in your conscious mind as well as your three higher bodies.

## How fallen beings distort vision

The first thing I would like to present to you is the concept of how the fallen beings have used vision and are using vision. You will, of course, see that there are a number of ideas in the world that are aimed at limiting people's vision, distorting their vision or guiding their vision into a certain track, a certain dead end, as we might say. I have talked about ideas that have a certain energetic hook built within them, but these ideas often form a filter. If you want to have a visual illustration, you may envision that in front of your vision, there is a device similar to a kaleidoscope.

You know that a kaleidoscope has certain panels inside of it with glass beads that the light shines through, and the light is colored by the glass. You know that these can be rearranged so they form various patterns. The ideas created by the fallen beings are like these panels in the kaleidoscope that distort your vision.

You also know that in a kaleidoscope you normally cannot see through, you cannot see anything on the other end. What I desire you to see here is that your three higher bodies, your identity, mental and emotional body, form a kind of kaleidoscope.

How is a kaleidoscope compared with binoculars? If the kaleidoscope was totally cleared from any colored glass patterns, you would be able to see clearly what the material world is like. Because you have certain colored patterns in the three higher bodies, your vision is limited and distorted, colored by these ideas that you hold. The fallen beings are very active and very aggressive in promoting ideas and constantly seeking to get people to believe in them. What I want to draw to your attention here is that the fallen beings actually have a much easier task than you might think.

If the fallen beings can get you over a certain hump, then they do not have to be concerned with you anymore. Your mind now becomes a closed circle that is a self-reinforcing limiting spiral, a downward spiral. The fallen beings no longer need to limit your vision because once *they* have pushed you over a certain hump, *you* are limiting your own vision.

## The purpose of expanding our sense of self

How does this happen? Well, let me explain to you something about how the material universe works. You understand that you are a spirit spark, you are a spiritual being. We have explained that what descends into the physical body, as an extension of the I AM Presence, is the Conscious You. We have said that this is pure awareness, meaning that it really does not have any built-in, inherent limitations. You can take on any role you want to play in the material universe, but you can also free yourself from the role because the Conscious You is not changed by the role. This is illustrated by my image of the kaleidoscope-binocular. The Conscious You is not changed by the panels that are put into the kaleidoscope. Its vision is changed, but the Conscious You itself is not changed. You can therefore remove the panels and clarify, purify, your vision anytime you want.

The purpose of the material universe is that Spirit – which you may call God or the Creator as you like, or you may call it an ascended being in the ascended realm – looks at this unascended sphere and sends an extension of itself into it. The purpose is that this extension starts out with a very limited, a very localized, sense of self. Through its interaction with the material world, this extension then expands its sense of self until it reaches the point where it can ascend from the unascended sphere and become an ascended master.

From there, you can continue to raise yourself to higher and higher levels of consciousness, up through the previous ascended spheres all the way to the Creator consciousness. When you reach that Creator consciousness, you now have the same awareness as your Creator, the same level of awareness and creativity. Because you were not created at this level, but have gone through the entire process of gradually growing, you have a much greater experience, a much greater awareness of how to express your creative abilities. This means that you are much better equipped to creating your own world than if you had not gone through this process.

If you had been created on a blank page, you would have had to experiment with your creative abilities and possibly make mistakes. The wisdom is that you start with much more limited creative abilities than that of a Creator so your mistakes are much more limited and much more easy to overcome. When I say "mistakes," I, of course, am using a word familiar to you. From the ascended state of consciousness, we do not look at it as mistakes but simply as experiments that were not a full expression of who you are. This, of course, applies to you as well in the material world. This is why we have no condemnation of you, the sense of shame and condemnation being created by the fallen beings.

## *The basis for a limited vision*

When you first descend as a new being into an unascended sphere, you have a very localized sense of self. At this point, you have, as the popular saying goes, only one way to go: "The only way to go is up." As you gain experiences in an unascended sphere, you gradually expand your sense of self. As Maitreya explains in his book, there comes a point where you need to no longer follow the teacher who is assisting you in expanding your sense of self. You come to the point where you need to become self-sufficient, and that means you need to experiment on your own instead of only doing what the teacher tells you to do.

It is, of course, at this point that you must face the initiation represented by the duality consciousness. This is the initiation where instead of seeing yourself as an extension of the hierarchy above you, as I have talked about in my previous discourses, you come to see yourself as an individual being, an isolated being, a separate being. You think you are creating on your own power, your own experience. Everyone must deal with this state of consciousness to some degree.

This does not mean you have to go into it and stay there and get lost in it. It is, of course, a possibility that some will choose to go into it. There is nothing inherently wrong with this, as it is just another experience. What can happen at this point is that you form a desire to go into a state of forgetting who you are and then from there, growing back to a higher awareness of who you are. Again, this is not wrong, this is simply another experience that is possible in an unascended sphere. This is a point where you can lose your conscious tie to your spiritual teacher and thereby lose your conscious awareness, your sense of identity of yourself as a connected being that is part of something greater than yourself.

How do you have this experience? As I said, you start out with a very localized sense of awareness, sense of self. You are aware that you are a part of something greater, you are connected to something. You start your creative efforts in a protected sphere where you are in constant contact with a spiritual teacher. This means that in the beginning phase of your growth in self-awareness, you are expanding your sense of self. You therefore come to a point where you have a greater sense of self than when you started. You also have a greater sense of self than what can be fit into the experience as a separate being.

How can the Conscious You go into what for most human beings on earth is the normal sense of self and experience that from the inside—and at the same time be completely convinced that this is real? How do you gain this sense of reality that you are a separate being, that you are living in a separate world where there is no direct connection to God and perhaps there is no God? How does this become real to you?

Well, it can become real only by limiting your vision. It is as I say, you start out with a binocular and then you put certain colored panes of glass in it that limit and distort your vision. Again, there is nothing wrong with this. This is actually not a fall; it is simply one possibility for expanding your self-awareness.

What you do as a co-creator is that you deliberately put yourself in a limited state in order to grow from there. You want to have the experience of going into an unascended sphere, taking on the body and mind of a human being on earth and at first being completely lost in that state. Again, when you do this, you are in a sense in the same situation as when you were first created: The only way to go is up. Being a human being on earth is such a limited state of consciousness that you really can only go up in self, or at least that is how it was in the original state.

The original intent that you had was that you would go into the identity as a human being and you would gradually expand on it until you were ready to ascend from the unascended sphere. What I am saying here is that in the original design, your original intention, you would gradually grow in self-awareness. You would constantly be moving up in self-awareness. You would start out with a limited vision and you would gradually purify your vision until you again saw yourself as part of the spiritual hierarchy above you.

What the fallen beings add to this mix, and what they added to the situation on earth after they were allowed to embody here, is that you can become stuck in the role, you can become stuck in the limited vision. Instead of constantly and gradually moving up to a purer and purer vision, you either get stuck at a certain level or you even start going down to a more and more limited vision.

## How current conditions limit our vision

When the earth was first created by the Elohim, there were many of the current conditions you see here that were not possible. This was because people who embodied on the earth at that time had a higher level of vision, a higher sense of self than what you see today.

It was not possible back then that human beings could descend to a sense of self where they were ready to kill other people and go to war and kill millions of other people. This, of course, is what you see today and this shows you that the fallen beings have been able to create this downward spiral. What they do is to use a combination of two kinds of beliefs.

First of all, there is the idea, which is very subtle and not found in overt form in most belief systems on earth, namely that you are a product of the material world or that you are in other ways imperfect. You are therefore a limited being by nature. You will notice that when you first decided to descend into an unascended sphere, even though you took on a very limited vision of yourself, you still knew that you were not limited to that sense of self. You knew you had the potential to expand it. What you see on earth today is that so many people have come to believe the subtle ideas of the fallen beings that a human being is defined by this or that limitation. You cannot rise above this, you are not on a path that systematically raises your sense of self and purifies your vision. You are either a sinner who must wait for some external savior to come and save you, or you are an evolved animal. So many people believe that they are inherently limited.

The second level of deception by the fallen beings is that there is nothing you can do about certain conditions on earth. You are inherently limited by them. This now means that human beings are put in a peculiar situation when it comes to vision. You first of all think that you are not capable of or worthy to consciously raise your vision. You also think that the current conditions on earth were not created by you and therefore there is nothing you can do to change them.

You cannot see beyond current conditions. You cannot see higher conditions as a realistic possibility. Your vision becomes a self-fulfilling downward spiral, a self-reinforcing downward spiral. You cannot raise your vision of yourself or of the world. This must, according to the force of the Mother, the contracting force, mean that you limit yourself even more. Once you have gotten beyond this hump, you are not susceptible, you are not open, to direct guidance from the ascended masters. You become susceptible to the School of Hard Knocks, and it is a matter of how limited your conditions need to be, how limited your vision needs to be, how intense your suffering needs to be, before you decide that this cannot be right and there must be a different approach.

As a spiritual student you, of course, are not entirely trapped in such a downward spiral. If you had been, you would not have been able to follow this course. You would have been far below the 48th level of consciousness and had no chance of raising yourself up. I am, again, in no way blaming you for your current lack of vision. As I have said before, it is my role to help you and I do not demand that you should be at such a level where you don't need my help before I will give you the help that it is my love and my joy to give you.

## Subtle ideas that limit vision

What I am pointing out to you is that you still have a need to purify your vision of many of these very, very subtle ideas that you have come to accept. What I hope you are beginning to understand, based on what I have said so far, is that some of these ideas are very subtle. There are so many conditions on earth that the vast majority of human beings do not even imagine that they could question. Do you see how incredibly limited most people are?

You have begun to question the sense that you are a sinner or that you are an evolved animal. You have realized that you are not either of these, you are a spiritual being. You do have the potential to raise your consciousness, to raise your sense of self. Can you begin to sense that just from growing up in a world that is as limited as the earth is, you have still come to accept a lot of conditions and limitations that you think are beyond questioning? You are now at the level where the natural next step for you is to start questioning some of these.

At this point, I need you to step up and realize that you have already started building an upward spiral. I said that most people are trapped in a self-reinforcing downward spiral that limits their vision. The fact that you have engaged in the spiritual path and have been following this course means that you have been building an upward spiral. So far, you may not have turned the corner where this upward spiral has become entirely self-sufficient.

I am not here saying that at this point you need to reach a level where you no longer need a teacher. We are obviously in the middle of this course of self-mastery and there are three Chohans above me who will take you towards the 96th level of consciousness. I *am* saying that there can come a point where you consciously realize that you need to expand your vision, that you want to expand your vision and that this means that you need to question the things that you take for granted. You need to question the things that you have not even thought about questioning and that most people have not thought about questioning. It will be much easier for yourself if you consciously recognize that this is actually what you want at this point.

As I said, I am from this point on in my retreat a facilitator. I do not force you; I do not confront you or put any pressure on you. I facilitate, but you must provide the driving power, the motivation, the desire. It will be helpful for you to make the switch in your conscious mind where you realize that you actually want to be free from a limited vision and that this can only be done by consciously questioning what most people do not question.

## 12 | Seeing Opportunities for Self-Transcendence

### How free will sets limits for what we can change

At this point, I need you to realize something about how free will works. You are living on a planet with more than seven billion other people. Each of these have a Conscious You that has free will. Through a very long and complicated process, each of the beings who are now in embodiment on earth have arrived at their current sense of self, their current vision. If you look at history, you will see that many more lifestreams have been embodied on earth over time. Throughout a very long time span, as Maitreya explains, human beings have been co-creating the current conditions on earth. For a substantial part of that time they have been influenced by the fallen beings.

As I have explained, this has led to the creation of certain secondary laws of nature. From the level of identity that most people have, from the fear-based state of consciousness that they have, these secondary laws of nature are insurmountable, there is no way to get around them. This is actually true. From *that* level of consciousness, there is no way to get around them. This has a very simple cause.

I have said that you cannot overcome your fear if your motivation for doing so is fear-based. Likewise, you cannot overcome your lack of vision with your current sense of vision—that is based on the current conditions you see in the material world. This is what forms a closed circle.

You have heard the popular expression that you cannot pull yourself up by your own bootstraps. Have you consciously thought about what it means? Imagine you are wearing a pair of boots that have straps on the side. You are standing on the floor, you stick your fingers through the straps on the side of your boots and now you pull up with all of your force. You realize, I am sure, that in order for you to actually exert the force that pulls up on your boot straps, your body has to create an equally strong force that is pushing down towards the floor. This is the mechanics of the material universe: action and re-action. For each action, there is an equally strong reaction with the opposite direction. When you have a vision that makes you think you are a human being and that the secondary laws of nature are insurmountable, then, of course, you cannot go beyond those secondary laws. Why can't you go beyond? Because you cannot see in your mind that it is possible to go beyond. Why can't you see this? Because you are looking through the kaleidoscope of your three higher bodies—and your conscious mind is at the bottom of the kaleidoscope.

We have said that the Conscious You is able to go into any role it wants to take on, experience it from the inside and experience it as perfectly real. For most people their Conscious You is centered in the physical body. When you are looking at the world, you are seeing through the contents of your three higher bodies but you are not realizing that you are seeing through them.

It is as if you are wearing colored glasses but you do not realize you are wearing colored glasses. From that perspective, you cannot question the contents of your three higher bodies, you cannot question what you see and realize it is distorted. This is why you cannot change anything. You cannot change the conditions that you think are created by the secondary laws of nature over which you have no power.

Here is where it becomes delicate and where it becomes necessary to carefully ponder this with the conscious mind. There are seven billion people in embodiment on earth. Most of them, the vast majority of them, have a very limited vision, a very limited sense of self. They accept the secondary laws of nature as insurmountable. They accept current conditions to a large degree as being beyond change. This is the experience that they are desiring to have right now. Most of them are not ready to go beyond this experience, they have not had enough of that experience.

As a spiritual being, you have your own individual free will, but you cannot override the free will of seven billion other people. There are certain conditions on earth that you individually cannot change. Even if you had the power to do so, it would violate the free will of those seven billion other people. How is it then possible for you to walk the spiritual path? It is possible, as I have said before, when you realize that there is no condition on earth that can prevent you from raising your consciousness. What I desire now is to have you step up and realize that it is not only that current conditions cannot prevent your growth, but that current conditions can actually facilitate your growth.

## How limitations can facilitate growth

Do you see, my beloved, that even as a spiritual student – or perhaps, *especially* as a spiritual student – you have become susceptible to what we have called the epic mindset of the fallen beings? If you look at human beings on earth, you will see that there are many of them that are living in a state of consciousness where they accept conditions on earth exactly as they are. They do not think there is anything wrong with it, that there is anything missing. They do not think that there is an epic battle between God and the devil and the current conditions are created by the devil. They are simply happily living their lives in the material world.

I am not saying this is something for which you should strive. I am only pointing out to you that they do not have the sense that things are wrong and must be changed. You do, of course, see that many religious, even many non-religious and especially many spiritual people have the mindset that something has gone wrong on earth, that something is missing, that these are not ideal conditions and that they should be changed.

Again, current conditions are not ideal conditions. They were not the conditions created by the Elohim, they do cause much suffering and, of course, it is the goal of the ascended masters to change them. However, our goal is to change them *within* the Law of Free will so that we seek to help and inspire people to raise their vision. It is not *us* who are changing conditions but people who do so through their higher vision. What you need to do in order to raise yourself to a higher level, in order to pass the initiations at the fifth level of my retreat, is to begin to question the entire epic mindset. You have, of course, to some degree done this already but what I specifically need you to question is the idea that current conditions are anti-spiritual and can prevent your spiritual growth.

The fallen beings have various levels of their strategy for keeping people in this closed circle, this self-reinforcing downward spiral. One is, of course, to keep them entirely focused on the material world and material pleasures. The people I am talking about who are happy about the material world and accepting current conditions (or perhaps some are not happy but still accepting current conditions) they are trapped at that level. They think there is nothing that can be done about it.

Then you have a higher level where people have started realizing that something is not right and something is missing. The fallen beings have then managed to trap them in the sense that there is an epic struggle between God and the devil and it is uncertain who is going to win.

As we have explained before, there is no epic struggle between God and the devil because God the Creator is not in any way affected by what is going on in an unascended sphere. That is why there is an unascended sphere where everything is like a sandbox and where anything created can easily be erased and nothing is permanent. The fallen beings could never create anything permanent that could oppose God. They want you to think that they have done so, and therefore they want you to be trapped in either battling them or feeling despair or hopelessness over the uncertainty of whether the world will be saved.

## *You can always transcend*

This is what I need you to step away from so you realize that, regardless of current conditions, the fallen beings or the conditions they have created cannot stop your self-transcendence. What is self-transcendence? In its essence, it is that you transcend the condition you are facing right now. It does not matter how low the current condition is, you can still transcend it. This is the lie that the fallen beings have been promoting in many different versions, namely, that there are conditions so low that you cannot use them for self-transcendence.

Do you see what I said earlier? When you first descended into the consciousness of seeing yourself as a separate being, you had a built-in sense that you could transcend your current sense of self, that you could go up. Most people on earth have come to believe the lie of the fallen beings that this is not possible. You, of course, have some sense that it is possible or you would not be on the path. You still have in your three higher bodies, many subtle beliefs that there are conditions that are not spiritual and do not facilitate your spiritual growth. This is a matter of vision. When you look at the world through the limiting beliefs in your three higher bodies, your total vision of the world is such that there are many conditions you think are not spiritual and will oppose your spiritual growth. If you look back at your life, if you look at your present beliefs, if you look at some of the spiritual teachings you have been studying and following, you will see that this idea lies as a very subtle backdrop for what most people believe and how they look at life. It is very, very subtle. There is at the lowest level the sense that there are conditions on earth that cannot be changed and that you cannot transcend. At the slightly higher level, where people are conscious of the spiritual path, there is still the sense that certain conditions are so that they cannot facilitate your spiritual growth. Therefore, you are trapped in either thinking that you must change those conditions or you must avoid them, you must run away from them.

What I am pointing out to you is simple: When you look at your life right now, I am sure there are certain conditions that you think you cannot change. It may be that you cannot change them because your vision is too limited. It may also be, as I have explained, that you cannot change them because doing so would violate the free will of the seven billion other people or of certain people in your family or society. You are part of a collective unit and the people in that collective unit have a certain vision. You cannot necessarily change these conditions.

## The subtle lie that you cannot transcend

What you *can* do is to change the way you look at those conditions so that you shift. Instead of seeing them as obstacles to your self-transcendence, you see them as opportunities, as the facilitators of your self-transcendence. Instead of looking at a condition, dreading it, regretting it, feeling hopeless about it, thinking: "Oh, I must change it, I must get away from this in order to be spiritual," you can now look at the condition and say: "Ah, what an opportunity to transcend myself." This is a monumental shift in self-awareness. Many people have been on the spiritual path for 30 or 40 years without making this shift. I am telling you that you are at the level of this course of self-mastery where you *can* make this shift, and I am here to help you. I will do everything I can when you are in my retreat in your finer bodies. What *you* can do is ponder these ideas with your conscious mind.

You can also formulate, or rather become aware of the fact that you already have, a love-based intention to make this shift. I have said that I do not want you to live the rest of your life fearing death and then only overcoming it on your death-bed. I do not want you to live the rest of your life while seeing conditions on earth as being the enemies of your spiritual growth when you could, in fact, make the shift into seeing them as opportunities.

Do you not see, my beloved, that the lie promoted by the fallen beings is very simple. There is first the belief that current conditions on earth are not the way they should be, they should be better. Then, there is the belief that you are a spiritual being, you are striving to be better, you are striving to go into a better world where conditions are higher than they are right now. You know that in order to go into this higher world, you have to transcend yourself. The lie promoted by the fallen beings is that there are certain conditions in this world that are so bad that you cannot use them for self-transcendence. You must either battle them and change them or you must seek to get away from them.

Do you not see what they are trying to say here? What is self-transcendence? It is that you realize that your current condition is less. You realize it is possible to be more and then you shift your sense of self away from less and to the more. Do you not see that the essence of self-transcendence is that you go from less to more? It does not matter how low the less is; you can always go to more. What the fallen beings are trying to make you believe is that there are certain lesser conditions that are so low that you cannot go from less to more.

Do you not see the lie? No matter how low it is, you can always go from less to more. In fact, the lower it is, the easier it becomes to go from less to more because the more there is a contrast between the condition you see with the outer mind and the reality, the higher reality, that you sense in your heart.

## *You already know that the lie is a lie*

Do you not see that the most difficult shifts on the spiritual path are the very subtle ones where you only see a small difference between the vision you have through your outer mind, through the kaleidoscope of the three lower bodies, and the inner vision, the intuitive vision, you have. Do you not see that what drives you on the spiritual path is that you do have some inner vision? You do have some intuitive, higher vision that comes from your I AM Presence and the ascended masters.

This is what gives you a sense that there is something more. At the same time, you are, of course, in your daily life looking through the kaleidoscope of your four lower bodies and you are seeing a much lower vision. What you have done so far is thinking that what you see from the intuitive vision is a higher reality that exists in a higher realm. This is correct, but what you have also done is thinking that what you see through the kaleidoscope of your four lower bodies is also a reality that exists in the material world.

The switch I am asking you to make is to realize that what you are seeing through the kaleidoscope of your four lower bodies is *not* a reality; *it is only a perception*. Other masters have talked about the same thing. Gautama Buddha has talked about perception, Maitreya talked about perception in his book, Mother Mary talked about perception in her Course on Abundance.

It is not that there isn't an external reality in the form of certain conditions in the material world. They are there, they are co-created by humankind, but you are not seeing those conditions. You are seeing an image and that image is produced in your four lower bodies.

In order to grow on the spiritual path, in order to raise your sense of self, you do not have to change the outer conditions. You only have to change the inner vision. You do not have to change anything outside yourself; you only have to purify your vision. When you purify your vision, when you purify the contents of your four lower bodies, you will begin to see the conditions in the material world as I see them. I do not see them as a threat or an obstacle to self-transcendence.

I have talked about the fact that there is a School of Hard Knocks and it is a matter of how hard the knocks have to become before people are awakened and want something more. Do you not see that in a sense the fallen beings can be said to be doing the ascended masters a favor by taking you lower and lower? The more dense and primitive conditions become, the greater the contrast becomes between what you see through the lower mind and what you know within. It is just a matter of when the gap becomes so big that people realize there must be another way to approach life.

I know that this is not an ideal condition. I am not trying to find excuses for the fallen beings or saying that they are just doing what they should be doing. I am not justifying the evil you see on earth. I am only pointing out to you, at this current level of initiation that you are at, that it is possible to make this switch in your mind where you realize that no condition you are facing is an obstacle to self-transcendence. It is a *facilitator* of self-transcendence.

## The Law of Self-Transcendence

Take a condition you are facing right now in your life that you think is, or that you have been thinking is, unspiritual or is an enemy of your spiritual growth. What I am pointing out to you is that you can make the shift so that you realize that this condition seems to be an obstacle only because you are looking at it through a particular sense of self. This self is made up of the conditions in your four lower bodies. If you think something is unspiritual, it shows that you have a limited sense of self that is based on an impure vision.

The very thing that you now think is an obstacle to your spiritual growth is actually the greatest opportunity for seeing your limited vision and starting to do something about it. There is a law that is in effect on earth, and the law could be said to define the condition for self-transcendence. It is that you will not escape any condition on earth until you fully accept it as it is and accept that it does not limit you as a spiritual being.

Do you see what the epic mindset has done to many spiritual people? Even the ascended master teachings are to some degree reinforcing this tendency when people first come in contact with our teachings. You think that you need to resist certain conditions; you need to not accept them. What I am saying is this: When you truly understand what I have told you, you understand that current conditions are created by people exercising their free will. God has given them the right to do this.

Other people have created certain conditions and they are affecting you, but other people have created these conditions through a limited sense of self. Why are these conditions affecting you? Because you have at least a certain element of that limited sense of self in your four lower bodies. Otherwise, you would not be affected by the conditions, you would not react to them, you would not react against them, you would not be disturbed or feel limited by them or feel they can hold back your spiritual growth. You would not even have a desire to change them. They would be inconsequential, irrelevant to you.

Do you not realize that there are many conditions on earth that you are not concerned about? You may have grown up in a world where it is natural that you have clean drinking water, but a very large percentage of the world's population cannot get clean drinking water out of their tap. They don't even have a tap, many of them. Why should you be concerned about this when you have grown up in a society where you don't have that problem?

What I am saying is that the conditions that are concerning you are no more limiting you in reality than these conditions that you consider irrelevant. It is a matter of making the switch where you realize that if you transcend the sense of self through which you have so far looked at the condition, then the condition will no longer disturb you.

## *Changing your mind can change outer conditions*

It doesn't mean that the condition will be changed because it is still upheld by the collective consciousness of other people, but it means that it will no longer limit you. In many cases, once you come to that point of transcending a certain condition by accepting that it is there, but that you are not affected by it, then you may find that your outer situation will actually change and you will move away from that condition.

As I said, this messenger decided that he wanted to transcend the sense of self that had attracted certain people to him and he does not attract those kind of people anymore. Many people have experienced the same thing. The same can be the case for outer physical conditions. It is amazing the changes that can happen in your life when you overcome the sense of self that makes you think you cannot be spiritual when certain conditions are there.

You can be spiritual regardless of the conditions you face. Many people have proven this throughout the centuries, throughout the ages. You are here to prove it in this age. *That* is why you volunteered to come into embodiment at this time. I am not telling you something you don't know within. I am reminding you so that you may make the switch in your conscious awareness and begin to look at your life and your outer situation with a new form of acceptance that this is a grand opportunity for self-transcendence.

Serapis Bey I AM, and I am transcending myself every second of every minute of every hour of every day. I am here to help you do the same. Take the hand that I reach out to you and we will together walk higher on this glorious path of self-transcendence offered to us by our Creator.

# 13 | INVOKING PURE VISION

In the name I AM THAT I AM, Jesus Christ, I call to my I AM Presence to flow through the I Will Be Presence that I AM and give this invocation with full power. I call to beloved Elohim Purity and Astrea and Cyclopea and Virginia, Archangel Gabriel and Hope and Raphael and Mother Mary, Serapis Bey and Hilarion to help me transcend all distorted vision. Help me see and surrender all patterns that block my oneness with Serapis Bey and with my I AM Presence, including …

[Make personal calls]

## Part 1

1. Serapis Bey, help me see how the fallen beings are limiting my vision through the illusions that form a filter in my identity, mental and emotional bodies.

> Beloved Astrea, your heart is so true,
> your Circle and Sword of white and blue,
> cut all life free from dramas unwise,
> on wings of Purity our planet will rise.
>
> **Beloved Astrea, in God Purity,**
> **accelerate all of my life energy,**
> **raising my mind into true unity**
> **with the Masters of love in Infinity.**

2. Serapis Bey, help me see any ideas that have turned my vision into a closed circle, a self-reinforcing spiral, so I am limiting my own vision.

> Beloved Astrea, from Purity's Ray,
> send forth deliverance to all life today,
> acceleration to Purity, I AM now free
> from all that is less than love's Purity.
>
> **Beloved Astrea, in oneness with you,**
> **your circle and sword of electric blue,**
> **with Purity's Light cutting right through,**
> **raising within me all that is true.**

3. Serapis Bey, help me experience myself as a spiritual being, as pure awareness, so I will know that while my vision is changed by the ideas in my four lower bodies, I myself am not changed and I can purify my vision any time.

> Beloved Astrea, accelerate us all,
> as for your deliverance I fervently call,
> set all life free from vision impure
> beyond fear and doubt, I AM rising for sure.

> **Beloved Astrea, I AM willing to see,
> all of the lies that keep me unfree,
> I AM rising beyond every impurity,
> with Purity's Light forever in me.**

4. Serapis Bey, help me pass the initiation represented by the duality consciousness and truly know that I am not a separate being and that I can create nothing of my own power.

> Beloved Astrea, accelerate life
> beyond all duality's struggle and strife,
> consume all division between God and man,
> accelerate fulfillment of God's perfect plan.

> **Beloved Astrea, I lovingly call,
> break down separation's invisible wall,
> I surrender all lies causing the fall,
> forever affirming the oneness of All.**

5. Serapis Bey, help me reestablish my conscious tie to my spiritual teacher and reclaim my sense of identity as a connected being that is part of something greater than myself.

> Cyclopea so dear, the truth you reveal,
> the truth that duality's ailments will heal,
> your Emerald Light is like a great balm,
> my emotional body is perfectly calm.

> **Cyclopea so dear, in Emerald Sphere,
> to vision so clear I always adhere,
> in raising perception I shall persevere,
> as deep in my heart your truth I revere.**

6. Serapis Bey, help me see how I limited my vision in order to have a sense of reality as a separate being. I consciously surrender the desire for the experience of going into an unascended sphere as a human being and being lost in that state. I want to fully awaken to my true identity.

> Cyclopea so dear, with you I unwind,
> all negative spirals clouding my mind,
> I know pure awareness is truly my core,
> the key to becoming the wide-open door.

> **Cyclopea so dear, clear my inner sight,**
> **empowered, I pierce the soul's fearful night,**
> **through veils of duality I now take flight,**
> **bathed in your penetrating Emerald Light.**

7. Serapis Bey, I consciously surrender the lie that I am a product of the material world, that I am imperfect and that I am a limited being by nature.

> Cyclopea so dear, life can only reflect,
> the images that my mind does project,
> the key to my healing is clearing the mind,
> from the images my ego is hiding behind.

> **Cyclopea so dear, I want to aim high,**
> **to your healing flame I ever draw nigh,**
> **I now see my life through your single eye,**
> **beyond all disease I AM ready to fly.**

8. Serapis Bey, I consciously surrender the lie that a human being is defined by limitations, cannot rise above them and cannot follow a path that systematically raises my sense of self and purifies my vision.

> Cyclopea so dear, your Emerald Flame,
> exposes every subtle, dualistic power game,
> including the game of wanting to say,
> that truth is defined in only one way.

> **Cyclopea so dear, I am feeling the flow,**
> **as your Living Truth upon me you bestow,**
> **I know truth transcends all systems below,**
> **immersed in your light, I continue to grow.**

9. Serapis Bey, I consciously surrender the lie that there is nothing I can do about certain conditions on earth, that I am inherently limited by them.

> Accelerate into Purity, I AM real,
> Accelerate into Purity, all life heal,
> Accelerate into Purity, I AM MORE,
> Accelerate into Purity, all will soar.

> Accelerate into Purity! (3X)
> Beloved Elohim Astrea.
> Accelerate into Purity! (3X)
> Beloved Gabriel and Hope.
> Accelerate into Purity! (3X)
> Beloved Serapis Bey.
> Accelerate into Purity! (3X)
> Beloved I AM.

## Part 2

1. Serapis Bey, help me see any self-reinforcing spirals that limit my vision and keep me trapped in the School of Hard Knocks.

> Gabriel Archangel, your light I revere,
> immersed in your Presence, nothing I fear.
> A disciple of Christ, I do leave behind,
> the ego's desire for responding in kind.
>
> **Gabriel Archangel, of this I am sure,**
> **Gabriel Archangel, Christ light is the cure.**
> **Gabriel Archangel, intentions so pure,**
> **Gabriel Archangel, in you I'm secure.**

2. Serapis Bey, help me start questioning the very subtle beliefs I have come to accept from growing up in the limited conditions found on earth, the conditions that people do not even imagine that they could question.

> Gabriel Archangel, I fear not the light,
> in purifications' fire, I delight.
> With your hand in mine, each challenge I face,
> I follow the spiral to infinite grace.
>
> **Gabriel Archangel, of this I am sure,**
> **Gabriel Archangel, Christ light is the cure.**
> **Gabriel Archangel, intentions so pure,**
> **Gabriel Archangel, in you I'm secure.**

3. Serapis Bey, help me see that I have already started building an upward spiral and help me turn the corner where this upward spiral becomes self-reinforcing.

## 13 | Invoking Pure Vision

> Gabriel Archangel, your fire burning white,
> ascending with you, out of the night.
> My ego has nowhere to run and to hide,
> in ascension's bright spiral, with you I abide.
>
> **Gabriel Archangel, of this I am sure,**
> **Gabriel Archangel, Christ light is the cure.**
> **Gabriel Archangel, intentions so pure,**
> **Gabriel Archangel, in you I'm secure.**

4. Serapis Bey, I consciously realize that I need to expand my vision, that I want to expand my vision. Help me question the things that I take for granted, that I have not even thought about questioning.

> Gabriel Archangel, your trumpet I hear,
> announcing the birth of Christ drawing near.
> In lightness of being, I now am reborn,
> rising with Christ on bright Easter morn.
>
> **Gabriel Archangel, of this I am sure,**
> **Gabriel Archangel, Christ light is the cure.**
> **Gabriel Archangel, intentions so pure,**
> **Gabriel Archangel, in you I'm secure.**

5. Serapis Bey, I do have the driving power, the motivation, the desire to be free from a limited vision. I know this can only be done by consciously questioning what most people do not question.

Raphael Archangel, your light so intense,
raise me beyond all human pretense.
Mother Mary and you have a vision so bold,
to see that our highest potential unfold.

**Raphael Archangel, for vision I pray,
Raphael Archangel, show me the way,
Raphael Archangel, your emerald ray,
Raphael Archangel, my life a new day.**

6. Serapis Bey, help me free myself from having my attention centered in the physical body where I am seeing through the contents of my three higher bodies and therefore cannot question the contents of those bodies.

Raphael Archangel, in emerald sphere,
to immaculate vision I always adhere.
Mother Mary enfolds me in her sacred heart,
from Mother's true love, I am never apart.

**Raphael Archangel, for vision I pray,
Raphael Archangel, show me the way,
Raphael Archangel, your emerald ray,
Raphael Archangel, my life a new day.**

7. Serapis Bey, help me accept that when I free my vision, I can free myself from the secondary laws of nature. However, I cannot override the free will of other people so there are certain conditions I cannot change.

## 13 | Invoking Pure Vision

> Raphael Archangel, all ailments you heal,
> each cell in my body in light now you seal.
> Mother Mary's immaculate concept I see,
> perfection of health is real now for me.
>
> **Raphael Archangel, for vision I pray,**
> **Raphael Archangel, show me the way,**
> **Raphael Archangel, your emerald ray,**
> **Raphael Archangel, my life a new day.**

8. Serapis Bey, help me fully accept that there is no condition on earth that can prevent me from raising my consciousness. Current conditions cannot prevent my growth, they can actually facilitate my growth.

> Raphael Archangel, your light is so real,
> the vision of Christ in me you reveal.
> Mother Mary now helps me to truly transcend,
> in emerald light with you I ascend.
>
> **Raphael Archangel, for vision I pray,**
> **Raphael Archangel, show me the way,**
> **Raphael Archangel, your emerald ray,**
> **Raphael Archangel, my life a new day.**

9. Serapis Bey, help me free myself from the epic mindset of the fallen beings, the mindset that something has gone wrong on earth, that something is missing, that these are not ideal conditions and that they should be changed.

With angels I soar,
as I reach for MORE.
The angels so real,
their love all will heal.
The angels bring peace,
all conflicts will cease.
With angels of light,
we soar to new height.

**The rustling sound of angel wings,**
**what joy as even matter sings,**
**what joy as every atom rings,**
**in harmony with angel wings.**

## Part 3

1. Serapis Bey, I consciously surrender the idea that current conditions are anti-spiritual and can prevent my spiritual growth. Self-transcendence is that I transcend the condition I am facing right now. It does not matter how low the current condition is, I can still transcend it.

Serapis Bey, what power lies,
behind your purifying eyes.
Serapis Bey, it is a treat,
to enter your sublime retreat.

**O Holy Spirit, flow through me,**
**I am the open door for thee.**
**O mighty rushing stream of Light,**
**transcendence is my sacred right.**

2. Serapis Bey, help me become aware of the fact that I already have a love-based intention to make this shift. I do not want to live the rest of my life while seeing conditions on earth as being the enemies of my spiritual growth. I want to make the shift into seeing them as opportunities.

> Serapis Bey, what wisdom found,
> your words are always most profound.
> Serapis Bey, I tell you true,
> my mind has room for naught but you.

> **O Holy Spirit, flow through me,**
> **I am the open door for thee.**
> **O mighty rushing stream of Light,**
> **transcendence is my sacred right.**

3. Serapis Bey, I consciously surrender the lie promoted by the fallen beings that there are certain conditions in this world that are so bad that I cannot use them for self-transcendence. I must either battle them or seek to get away from them.

> Serapis Bey, what love beyond,
> my heart does leap, as I respond.
> Serapis Bey, your life a poem,
> that calls me to my starry home.

> **O Holy Spirit, flow through me,**
> **I am the open door for thee.**
> **O mighty rushing stream of Light,**
> **transcendence is my sacred right.**

4. Serapis Bey, I consciously see that self-transcendence is that I realize my current condition is less and it is possible to be more. Then, I shift my sense of self away from less and to the more. The essence of self-transcendence is that I go from less to more.

> Serapis Bey, your guidance sure,
> my base is clear and white and pure.
> Serapis Bey, no longer trapped,
> by soul in which my self was wrapped.
>
> **O Holy Spirit, flow through me,**
> **I am the open door for thee.**
> **O mighty rushing stream of Light,**
> **transcendence is my sacred right.**

5. Serapis Bey, I consciously see that it does not matter how low the less is; I can always go to more. The lower a condition is, the easier it becomes to see the contrast between the condition and the higher reality I sense in my heart.

> Serapis Bey, what healing balm,
> in mind that is forever calm.
> Serapis Bey, my thoughts are pure,
> your discipline I shall endure.
>
> **O Holy Spirit, flow through me,**
> **I am the open door for thee.**
> **O mighty rushing stream of Light,**
> **transcendence is my sacred right.**

6. Serapis Bey, help me make the most difficult shifts on the spiritual path, namely the very subtle ones where I only see a small difference between the vision I have through my outer mind and my inner vision.

> Serapis Bey, what secret test,
> for egos who want to be best.
> Serapis Bey, expose in me,
> all that is less than harmony.

> **O Holy Spirit, flow through me,**
> **I am the open door for thee.**
> **O mighty rushing stream of Light,**
> **transcendence is my sacred right.**

7. Serapis Bey, I consciously see that I do have some inner vision, I do have some intuitive, higher vision that comes from my I AM Presence and the ascended masters.

> Serapis Bey, what moving sight,
> my self ascends to sacred height.
> Serapis Bey, forever free,
> in sacred synchronicity.

> **O Holy Spirit, flow through me,**
> **I am the open door for thee.**
> **O mighty rushing stream of Light,**
> **transcendence is my sacred right.**

8. Serapis Bey, I consciously surrender the lie that what I see from the intuitive vision is a higher reality that exists only in a higher realm. I now see that it is also a reality that exists in the material world.

Serapis Bey, you balance all,
the seven rays upon my call.
Serapis Bey, in space and time,
the pyramid of self, I climb.

**O Holy Spirit, flow through me,
I am the open door for thee.
O mighty rushing stream of Light,
transcendence is my sacred right.**

9. Serapis Bey, I consciously realize that what I am seeing through the kaleidoscope of my four lower bodies is not a reality; it is only a perception. I am seeing an image that is produced in my four lower bodies.

Serapis Bey, your Presence here,
filling up my inner sphere.
Life is now a sacred flow,
God Purity I do bestow.

**O Holy Spirit, flow through me,
I am the open door for thee.
O mighty rushing stream of Light,
transcendence is my sacred right.**

## Part 4

1. Serapis Bey, I consciously see that in order to grow on the spiritual path, I do not have to change the outer conditions. I only have to change the inner vision. I do not have to change anything outside yourself; I only have to purify my vision.

## 13 | Invoking Pure Vision

> Hilarion, on emerald shore,
> I'm free from all that's gone before.
> Hilarion, I let all go,
> that keeps me out of sacred flow.

> **O Holy Spirit, flow through me,**
> **I am the open door for thee.**
> **O mighty rushing stream of Light,**
> **transcendence is my sacred right.**

2. Serapis Bey, help me make the switch in my mind where I realize that no condition I am facing is an obstacle to self-transcendence. It is a facilitator of self-transcendence. A condition seems to be an obstacle only because I am looking at it through a particular sense of self.

> Hilarion, the secret key,
> is wisdom's own reality.
> Hilarion, all life is healed,
> the ego's face no more concealed.

> **O Holy Spirit, flow through me,**
> **I am the open door for thee.**
> **O mighty rushing stream of Light,**
> **transcendence is my sacred right.**

3. Serapis Bey, I consciously see that the very thing that I have thought is an obstacle to my spiritual growth is actually the greatest opportunity for seeing my limited vision and transcending it.

Hilarion, your love for life,
helps me surrender inner strife.
Hilarion, your loving words,
thrill my heart like song of birds.

**O Holy Spirit, flow through me,
I am the open door for thee.
O mighty rushing stream of Light,
transcendence is my sacred right.**

4. Serapis Bey, I consciously see the Law of Self-Transcendence, which says that I will not escape any condition on earth until I fully accept it as it is and accept that it does not limit me as a spiritual being.

Hilarion, invoke the light,
your sacred formulas recite.
Hilarion, your secret tone,
philosopher's most sacred stone.

**O Holy Spirit, flow through me,
I am the open door for thee.
O mighty rushing stream of Light,
transcendence is my sacred right.**

5. Serapis Bey, I see that other people have created certain conditions that are affecting me, but they have done so through a limited sense of self. I am affected only because I have a certain element of that limited self in my four lower bodies.

## 13 | Invoking Pure Vision

Hilarion, with love you greet,
me in your temple over Crete.
Hilarion, your emerald light,
my third eye sees with Christic sight.

**O Holy Spirit, flow through me,
I am the open door for thee.
O mighty rushing stream of Light,
transcendence is my sacred right.**

6. Serapis Bey, help me make the switch where I realize that if I transcend the sense of self through which I have so far looked at the condition, then the condition will no longer disturb me.

Hilarion, you give me fruit,
of truth that is so absolute.
Hilarion, all stress decrease,
as my ambitions I release.

**O Holy Spirit, flow through me,
I am the open door for thee.
O mighty rushing stream of Light,
transcendence is my sacred right.**

7. Serapis Bey, I accept that I can be spiritual regardless of the conditions I face. Many people have proven this throughout the centuries, and I am here to prove it in this age. That is why I volunteered to come into embodiment at this time.

Hilarion, my chakras clear,
as I let go of subtlest fear.
Hilarion, I am sincere,
as freedom's truth I do revere.

> O Holy Spirit, flow through me,
> I am the open door for thee.
> O mighty rushing stream of Light,
> transcendence is my sacred right.

8. Serapis Bey, I am making the shift in my conscious awareness, and I look at my life and my outer situation with a new form of acceptance that this is a grand opportunity for self-transcendence.

> Hilarion, you balance all,
> the seven rays upon my call.
> Hilarion, you keep me true,
> as I remain all one with you.

> O Holy Spirit, flow through me,
> I am the open door for thee.
> O mighty rushing stream of Light,
> transcendence is my sacred right.

9. Serapis Bey, I am taking the hand that you reach out to me, and we will together walk higher on this glorious path of self-transcendence offered to us by our Creator.

> Hilarion, your Presence here,
> filling up my inner sphere.
> Life is now a sacred flow,
> God Vision I on all bestow.

> O Holy Spirit, flow through me,
> I am the open door for thee.
> O mighty rushing stream of Light,
> transcendence is my sacred right.

## Sealing:

In the name of the Divine Mother, I fully accept that the power of these calls is used to set free the Ma-ter light, so it can outpicture the perfect vision of Christ for my own life, for all people and for the planet. In the name I AM THAT I AM, it is done! Amen.

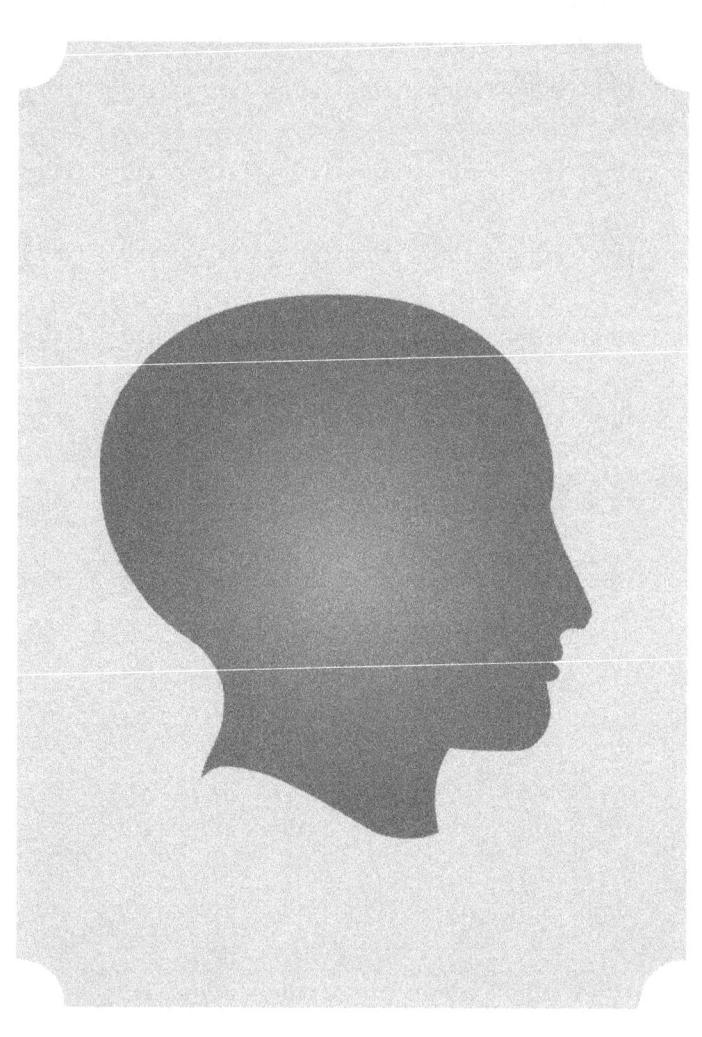

# 14 | FINDING PEACE IN GIVING SERVICE

I AM the Ascended Master Serapis Bey. We are now at the sixth level of my retreat, the level where you face the combination of the Fourth Ray of Purity and the Sixth Ray, which has often been called the ray of service and the ray of peace.

What is the connection between service and peace? We have told you that you descended to earth with a higher purpose, a purpose that is beyond what most people can see with their conscious minds. You descended here because you saw that this is a low planet with much darkness and that conditions need to be changed on earth. You came here because you thought that by taking embodiment, bringing your light, expressing your individual creativity, you could make a difference and indeed help raise the earth to a higher level where it can spin off some of the darker manifestations you currently see, such as war and other forms of man's inhumanity to man.

We might say that a huge part of your motivation, your intention, for coming to earth was to give a service that would help bring the earth to a higher level. It is therefore built into your deepest intention that you want to improve the earth, to raise up the earth.

## When service takes away your peace

What I aim to show you now is how your desire to give service to earth can take away your sense of peace. This is unfortunately something that can be reinforced by you finding the spiritual path and following a spiritual teaching. There are various spiritual teachings out there that are influenced by the subtle ideas of the fallen beings, especially the epic mindset. These teachings will directly give their followers the sense that they are here to change specific conditions on earth. Even the ascended master teachings, that we give, can reinforce this epic mindset and a desire to see specific changes on earth. We are, of course, often asking you to make calls for specific changes. Mother Mary's book on war, for example, gives you tools for making specific calls that will help eradicate war from the earth (*Help the Ascended Masters Stop War*). How, then, do you balance the desire to see specific changes with your inner peace?

It is obvious that we of the ascended masters want to see specific changes on earth. We obviously want to see war banished from this planet. We want to see the earth accelerated into a higher state where war and the lifestreams who embody the warring consciousness are simply spun off because they cannot remain with the accelerated vibration of the planet and the collective consciousness.

Nevertheless, as I said before, we want to see this within the context of the Law of Free Will. We want to see that a majority of the people on earth use their free will to raise their consciousness beyond the consciousness of, for example, war.

## 14 | Finding Peace in Giving Service

How can they do this? They *cannot* do so by being forced to do so.

Do you not see, my beloved, that we are not asking you to make calls and invocations that are forcing people? We are asking you to make calls that are raising their insight, their knowledge, their vision so that they can voluntarily make these changes.

Do you not see by now that one of the essential differences between the ascended masters and the false hierarchy is that we have total respect for free will and the false hierarchy have no respect for free will whatsoever.

## The fallen beings force people to react

What is it that the fallen beings have done from the moment they came to earth? They have forced people into reacting to them and against them. Do you not see that this is one of the mechanisms behind war and all kinds of violence? You are in a physical body, you have to live somewhere in order to exist and provide for yourself and your family. You live on a piece of land, if some other group of people assemble an army and come marching into your territory in order to take it over and potentially kill you and your family, then you are forced to react to that in some way.

This is how the fallen beings have forced people into these reactionary spirals that become self-reinforcing. You see, for example, in the Middle East how people have, for thousands of years, been trapped in the same kind of reactionary spiral. The fallen beings hardly need to do anything to keep it going because the people are doing so of their own accord. They cannot pull themselves out of these spirals. You see, of course, that these spirals are the antithesis to peace. There can be no peace among people when they are trapped in such a spiral. There can be no peace within people when they are trapped in such a spiral. These spirals that take away people's peace may not be warring among nations or ethnic groups. They can be spirals within families or at workplaces where you are, again, trapped in reacting to or reacting against other people. Some people, whether it be in their marriage or among their brothers and sisters or parents, have been trapped in a spiral with the same souls for lifetimes. They keep reincarnating in the same family groups because they cannot break out of the spirals they have with the other souls in the group.

You, of course, are a spiritual student, an ascended master student. You have already pulled yourself out of the more obvious of these reactionary spirals or you would not have raised yourself above the 48th level of consciousness. What I am seeking to help you see here is that there are other reactionary spirals that are more subtle.

One of these spirals is the sense that because the fallen beings have forced people into a downward spiral, you who are the spiritual people are justified in forcing people out of the downward spiral for their own good. This is the essence of the epic mindset where you think there is an epic battle between good and evil and you are taking the side of good. Because evil is so aggressive, it is necessary for you to use force to defeat evil or to free people from the clutches of evil.

This is the justification behind all the kinds of force-based measures taken by religious people, spiritual people or other types of well-meaning people who thought they were working for a good cause but were still using force. At your level, at the sixth level of my retreat on the Fourth Ray, you have freed yourself from these spirals, but have you completely freed yourself from the subtle mindset behind it?

## Service and success

Even if you are not reacting directly against other people or seeking to force them, you can still be affected by this subtle sense that you are here to give a service to earth and that the measure for evaluating whether you are successful in giving this service is that you see specific outer changes. My beloved, as long as you think that your service on this planet depends on producing specific outer changes that are tied to the free-will choices of other people, then you can never attain inner peace.

You may say, as many students do when we discuss this at the etheric level: "But Serapis, are you saying we are not here to give service and produce specific changes? Are we not here to help remove evil from the earth?" Well, the answer to that question is: "yes and no" because it depends on how you look at it.

We have before used the image that you can have a group of people who are trapped in a dark cave. Because they are in darkness, they cannot see where they are or what they are doing so there are certain choices they cannot make consciously. If you slowly increase the level of light in the room, the people will gradually begin to see more clearly. As their vision clears, they will, from within, begin to make more conscious, more aware choices. It has been said by Master MORE that if people knew better, they would do better and it is true for all except the fallen beings. It is even true for the fallen beings, but they will never get to know better until they shift their consciousness and swallow their pride, which is very difficult for them to do.

For all other lifestreams, if they truly see that there is a better option than what they have chosen so far, then they will, in most cases spontaneously, choose that option. As the old story goes, if you think you are holding a rope and the light increases and you see that it is a snake, you will spontaneously let go of the snake.

Your job is not to produce specific changes by forcing other people. How do you, for example, force people to become peaceful? It is force that takes away their peace and makes them go to war with each other. How does more force remove the force that is already there and has created havoc on earth? It cannot be done!

The fallen beings have created all kinds of subtle ideas that say, not only that it can be done but that it is the only way it can be done. The end can justify the means. This has never been and never will be the method of the ascended masters. We work with free will, within the Law of Free Will. Increase the light and people *will* make better choices. If they do not, then stand back and let them go into a downward spiral until they have had enough of that experience and cry out for more, as they inevitably will when the knocks become hard enough.

Can you see, my beloved, that there is a conflict between your original, pure love-based motivation for coming to earth and the motivation and the view that you have in your conscious mind and in your three higher bodies? Can you see that what I am pointing out to you is that as long as there is a conflict between the two, you cannot find inner peace on this planet?

You cannot be at peace with being in embodiment on earth as long as you think you are here to produce specific changes that are dependent on the free-will choices of other people. You must come to the point where you realize that your service to life does not depend on any condition or any person outside yourself.

When we discuss this at my retreat, when we sit in groups and discuss this topic, students often react by saying: "But how do we then give service? We cannot see how we give service." What have we said is the goal of the path of self-mastery? It is to be an open door for the light that comes from your I AM Presence and from the hierarchy of ascended masters above you.

## *The fallen beings fear your light*

The fallen beings desperately want you to believe that you are not allowed to express that light here on earth, that you cannot express that light, that you cannot express the light until certain conditions are fulfilled in your outer situation. They have so many layers of deception aimed at preventing you from doing the one thing you came here to do—being an open door for the light.

At the lowest level they do not want you to know that this is even an option. Then, they want you to think that it violates the free will of other people, especially themselves, if you express your light. If people want to live in darkness, they should be allowed to do so and you have no right to come here and express your light.

You see, my beloved, you *have* the right because you have taken physical embodiment. Your free will has become part of the equation on earth. I have said in a previous discourse that your individual free will cannot override the free will of the seven billion other people on the planet. This is true, but the reverse is also true. The free will of the seven billion other people on this planet cannot override your individual free will.

You have a right to be in embodiment, to be who you are and to be an open door for the light from the hierarchy above you. This is your God-given right. The fallen beings have a right to deny the light within themselves and deny the light within you. They do not have the right to demand that you should shut off your light. Actually, they do have a right to demand it, but you have no obligation to follow their demand.

On an even higher level of deception, they want you to think that expressing your light is something you cannot do until certain conditions are fulfilled. People need to be ready for it, you need to have certain outer conditions—enough money, a certain place to live, a peaceful environment, this or that condition.

What I have tried to take you through in the previous lessons is this process of seeing that there are no outer conditions that can prevent you from transcending yourself and therefore expressing more and more light. The fallen beings also want you to think that you cannot express your light because of certain inner conditions.

## Perfectionism is an invention of the fallen beings

We have talked about the fact that when you first came to earth, you experienced a birth trauma because the fallen beings brutally and aggressively rejected you, your individuality and your light. They made you feel in some way that you should not express this light, that you were rejected, that you were not good enough, that you have to be perfect in order to express your light.

Perfectionism is an invention of the fallen beings. They have taken the linear mind and done something that you should be very careful about doing with the linear mind. You see, the linear mind is linear because it always works with a progression. An example is, of course numbers where you count from 1, 2, 3, 4, and so on. There is always a progression, there is always a scale, and the linear mind wants to fit everything on such a scale. There are times where you can take the linear mind to its extreme in order to show the limitations of the linear mind. What the fallen beings have done is to take the linear mind to an extreme and say that God must be the highest possible being that can be imagined. This means that God is in a state of what they call perfection, a state where nothing changes.

The linear mind, of course, is always looking at change. There is always a progression, not only in numbers but also in time. Time is the child of the linear mind where it always progresses from one stage to the next. You take this progression to its ultimate extreme and you say: "Well, there must be something that never changes and when something is changing from less to more, that shows that the less is imperfect. Therefore, there must come a point where you have reached the ultimate state of more where things are perfect."

This, of course, is a lie. God is not perfect in the sense that God is not changing, for the Creator is constantly growing. That is why the Creator created you, me and all the rest of us. There is no state of non-change in any world that has form. If you want non-change, you need to go beyond any world that has form, and this is something that the fallen beings cannot even fathom. Therefore, they have created, as a replacement, the idea of perfection.

When you came and expressed your light, and when they felt threatened by it, they said: "Here on earth we have defined a standard for how you should behave. Your expression of your light does not live up to our standard and therefore you should not express your light here." They, of course, did not do this by saying that there was anything wrong with your light. They did it by saying there was something wrong with *you*. *You* did not live up to some kind of standard. This has caused many spiritual and religious people to put themselves on a path where they think they are working towards having this state of perfection. Many spiritual people have used the spiritual teachings and spiritual techniques and they strive to perfect themselves, the outer self, so that it lives up to the standard of the world. The thought that has been inserted into your mind is that when *you* become "perfect," *they* will accept your light. There are two lies here, actually more, but the two primary ones are that you will never become perfect because there is no state of perfection. Second, the fallen beings will never accept the light no matter how it is expressed. Beyond that is, of course, the lie that your light has to be accepted in order to do its work.

## Light will always do its work

You see, my beloved, what have I talked about as the cause of change? It is that the light is increased so that people can see more. Imagine, again, that you have a dark cave. This may be a cave with a tall ceiling and on the floor level many individual, different compartments and rooms. Almost like what you see in an office landscape where you have little cubicles where people are sitting in front of their computers. You know that in such an office building, if you increase the light by placing a lamp in one cubicle, then all of the other people cannot see that lamp. But it still increases the level of light in the room so that they can see more than they could see before.

What I am saying here is this: In order for your service to be successful, people do not even need to see that it is you who is expressing light, they do not need to accept you or your light, they do not need to acknowledge and recognize it. You just need to express your light and then let the light do its work.

What I am seeking to take you to here is a recognition in your conscious mind of the realization I seek to give you at

## 14 | Finding Peace in Giving Service

my retreat, namely that the success of your service does not depend on the reaction of other people. As long as you think it depends upon the reaction other people, you cannot be at peace—and here is the catch-22.

If you are not at peace with being in embodiment on earth, then you cannot be an open door for the Light while you are in embodiment on earth. This cannot be done!

You must be at peace in order to give service. In order to be at peace, you must disconnect your idea of service from the desire to produce specific results or be acknowledged, recognized and validated by other people. This brings me to a topic that is quite subtle.

### The impossible quest for fear-based self-esteem

You know, if you have paid attention to conditions on earth, that in recent decades there have been many groups of people who have gained more public awareness and more public recognition. You know that there are many minority groups that used to be kind of outcasts in society. They have now stood up and claimed their rights and gained so much attention that they have received more wide-spread recognition and acceptance than before.

You will know, if you look at the psychology of such people, that when you feel like a minority group and you feel like a downtrodden, outcast minority, you can have a low self-esteem, a low sense of self-worth. Well, when you first came to this planet, you came here with a healthy, love-based sense of self-worth. When you were brutally rejected by the fallen beings, you lost that sense of self-worth, at least some of it. You came to feel that you were an outcast, that you were not accepted, that you were not acceptable.

This put you in one of these catch-22s, one of these self-reinforcing downward spirals, that the fallen beings are so expert at creating. When you lost your sense of self-esteem and self-worth, you felt it as a lack. This is going into a fear-based state of mind. The essence of the fear-based state of mind is that you feel a lack, and therefore you develop a desire to compensate for the lack, to fill the lack. There is no way to fill the lack in a fear-based state of mind. It is a black hole that can never be filled.

What the sense of lack does is give you a desire to recapture your former self-worth. Unfortunately, you have now come to believe the lie of the fallen beings that you have to do this by gaining recognition and acceptance on earth—or, rather, recognition and acceptance from *them*. Can you not see the impossibility here? It was the fallen beings who destroyed your self-worth by rejecting you, and now you are trapped in a spiral of seeking to get them to accept you. They were the ones who created the lack of self-worth. What is the likelihood that they can fill it?

They will just keep feeding this spiral by, as you know, moving the goalpost further and further away so you never reach it. That is the whole purpose of the idea of perfection. Who can define perfection? Well, you may define it one way right now but when you reach that level, you will find that your self-worth is still not restored. What is the conclusion? It is that with the linear mind you can always define a higher level. How high can you count? When does the string of numbers end? Well, scientists do not know.

When will you ever be perfect in the minds of the fallen beings? Well, "never," my beloved. How long do you want to chase this carrot, dangling in front of the nose of the donkey pulling the cart where the fallen ones are sitting, laughing? Stop being the donkey for the fallen beings and instead be the open door for the light of the ascended masters!

## Ego-based motivation for walking the path

What is the switch you need to make? It is to recognize that when you find the spiritual path, you do not instantly get rid of your ego. There will be a period on your path where part of the motivation, part of the intention, for walking the path is supplied by the ego. The ego wants something.

Ideally, the ego would like to prevent you from even starting the path of self-mastery. When it cannot do that, as it truly cannot, given that you are reading this book, then it will want to get something out of you walking the path. When you look honestly at many spiritual people and spiritual movements and gurus, you will see a clear tendency.

As I said, those who are spiritual today are in most cases people who came to earth with a positive purpose of bringing their light and making a difference. When they were brutally rejected, they lost their self-worth and came to feel as outcasts. When you find a spiritual movement, you feel that here is a chance to recapture your self-esteem.

Many spiritual people – that are today members of spiritual movements, including ascended master movements – have felt like outcasts while they were growing up in a society that is often anti-spiritual. You then find a spiritual guru or teaching, and all of a sudden your ego now gains an opportunity for using this to build the sense that even though you are different from other people, this does not mean you are lower than them. In fact, you being different means that you are higher than them because you had a higher spiritual awareness. This is why you can recognize this teaching that most people cannot recognize.

I am not saying that it is not true that you have a higher level of awareness than most people on earth. Can you not see that it is not constructive for you to allow your ego to take you into this quest for using your spiritual teaching to reinforce the ego's desire to be special, to be better than others? The ego, as we have said many times, is a relative faculty and that means it compares everything to something else. It can, of course, only compare it to what it can see, and the ego can see only what is in duality. Duality is based on a value judgment; something is better than what is worse. The ego will always try to insert the belief that those who are the special people – because they are members of this particular spiritual organization and recognize the teachings of this special enlightened guru – are better than other people on earth.

My beloved, again, I am in no way blaming you. It is almost impossible to grow up on planet earth as it is today without being affected by this pattern. There are hardly any students who come to my retreat that do not have this pattern in their three higher bodies and often in their conscious mind as well. I am not here to blame you, I am not here to shame you. I am here to help you transcend the very pattern that takes away your inner peace.

You do recognize consciously, don't you, that you want inner peace and you want to be successful in giving your service on this planet? You want to serve in peace and you want the peace of knowing that your service is successful. When you recognize that this is what you want, then you do not need to resist me exposing the pattern in your mind that prevents you from having what you want. This desire to use the spiritual teaching to set yourself above other people, *will* take away your inner peace.

I realize that for some people it has given them a superficial sense of peace. If you look at the many spiritual movements on earth, you will see that there are many of them that follow the same pattern. They have a spiritual teaching, they have a spiritual guru who is either alive or who has now moved on from the physical plane. They idolize this guru and make him or her seem very special. The more special the guru is, the more special *they* become for following this guru. After all, the vast majority of the people on this planet did not recognize the guru, just as most people did not recognize Jesus or the Buddha while they were here. The fact that *you* recognize the guru, must mean that you are very special. The fewer there are of you that are so special, the more special you become compared to so many other people who could not recognize your guru.

There are people who sit there and have created a self-reinforcing spiral where they validate each other in being so special. They can even attain a certain superficial sense of being at peace in being so special and doing exactly what they should be doing by isolating themselves in this ivory tower. Well, if you had been trapped completely in one of these spirals, you would not have been reading this. The fact that you *are* reading this means that you have already started freeing yourself from it. All that is left in order to be completely free is that you consciously see the mechanism and consciously let it go.

## *You are special and unique*

My beloved, I am talking to you individually. *You* are special, *you* are unique. But your uniqueness is not anchored in your four lower bodies. Your uniqueness is anchored in your I AM Presence and causal body and in the Conscious You that is an extension of your Presence.

What you have attempted to do down here on earth is to build an outer self that is special compared to other people. This can never fill your desire to recapture your self-worth. You can never feel completely at peace as long as you are comparing yourself to anything in an unascended octave, in an unascended sphere. The only way to recapture your sense of self-worth – to feel at peace with being who you are, to feel at peace with expressing who you are on earth – is to reconnect to the fact that your specialness is in your God-given individuality, not in the individuality you have built as a reaction to the conditions created by the fallen beings.

Why do you need to gain the recognition of the fallen beings or other human beings when you have the recognition of your Creator and the ascended masters? You may say, as many students say at my retreat: "But it is because in our conscious minds we can feel the recognition from other people but we cannot feel the recognition from you and from God." This is true, but it is only true because you have not made a shift in your conscious mind that allow you to feel our recognition. Our recognition and validation of you, our love for you, is constantly raining upon you from above.

How do you become an ascended master? By becoming the open door for the love that is streaming through you from an even higher level to a lower level. I AM the Chohan of the Fourth Ray. I am not producing the light of the Fourth Ray, I am tied in to the source of that light, that goes all the way back to the Creator. I am in that flow, I am an open door for that flow. I can direct it, but it is my joy to let it flow through me. I am constantly letting the light flow through me in order to experience ultimate joy.

Why would I limit my joy by holding back the light from you? I am not the one who is limiting the light that streams to you. *You* are the one who does not recognize the light because you have some limitation in your mind that makes you think you are not worthy of it or not capable of receiving it. *That* is what I aim to help you change at the sixth level of my retreat.

My aim is to help you know at the level of your identity body that you are unique. You are not unique in comparison to others because in the ascended realm comparisons are meaningless, they simply do not exist. You are unique in an incomparable way. The concern about whether you are better or worse than anybody else is completely obsolete and irrelevant. When you know this in your identity body, you can gradually bring it down towards your mental and emotional bodies and then towards your conscious mind. If you will, you may be able to switch and even for a second experience my love.

After you give the invocation based on this chapter, perhaps sit still for a time and just tune in to my Presence and be open to experiencing my love. If you can experience this consciously, it can bring about a shift. You will be able to accept that you are unique, you are special. You are worthy the way God created you. You do not need to be unique, special or worthy compared to anything on earth, any standard on earth. You do not need to be better than other people and therefore you do not need to put them down.

Do you not see, my beloved, that in these communities I am talking about (where they are sitting around validating each other as being so special) they actually have an extremely judgmental attitude. Anyone who does not live up to the conditions defined in their community automatically becomes judged and becomes an outcast. You cannot be a part of that community unless you are willing to validate all others and validate their specialness. If you question it, you will be frozen out or thrown out. This is fear-based, and what I desire to see for you is that you find a love-based sense of self-worth and that sense of self-worth is already there. It is not a matter of developing it, acquiring it. It is only a matter of opening yourself up to experiencing it and accepting it. Accepting that this is who you are and you are worthy.

How can you feel at peace on earth unless you know that you are worthy and that your worthiness comes from a source that is beyond anything on earth? I do not desire to see you live the rest of your life in a state of not being at peace and then, just before you pass from the screen of life, you have that moment of clarity where you see that by making a simple switch, you could have lived your entire life being at peace. I do not desire you to make that shift at the end of your life.

I desire you to make that shift *right now* so that you can live the rest of your life in peace, knowing that you are performing the greatest service you can perform by being who you are, by being an open door for the light that you are.

I AM an open door for the Light that I AM. Can you feel my light? It is the same light that is in you.

Serapis Bey I AM.

# 15 | INVOKING PEACE IN SERVICE

In the name I AM THAT I AM, Jesus Christ, I call to my I AM Presence to flow through the I Will Be Presence that I AM and give this invocation with full power. I call to beloved Elohim Purity and Astrea and Peace and Aloha, Archangel Gabriel and Hope and Uriel and Aurora, Serapis Bey and Nada to help me transcend all desires for service that take away my peace. Help me see and surrender all patterns that block my oneness with Serapis Bey and with my I AM Presence, including …

[Make personal calls]

## Part 1

1. Serapis Bey, help me see my motivation for coming to earth, my desire to give a service that would help bring the earth to a higher level.

Beloved Astrea, your heart is so true,
your Circle and Sword of white and blue,
cut all life free from dramas unwise,
on wings of Purity our planet will rise.

**Beloved Astrea, in God Purity,
accelerate all of my life energy,
raising my mind into true unity
with the Masters of love in Infinity.**

2. Serapis Bey, help me see how my desire to give service to earth can take away my sense of peace.

Beloved Astrea, from Purity's Ray,
send forth deliverance to all life today,
acceleration to Purity, I AM now free
from all that is less than love's Purity.

**Beloved Astrea, in oneness with you,
your circle and sword of electric blue,
with Purity's Light cutting right through,
raising within me all that is true.**

3. Serapis Bey, help me see if I have used a spiritual teaching to reinforce the epic mindset and a desire to see specific changes on earth.

Beloved Astrea, accelerate us all,
as for your deliverance I fervently call,
set all life free from vision impure
beyond fear and doubt, I AM rising for sure.

## 15 | Invoking Peace in Service

**Beloved Astrea, I AM willing to see,
all of the lies that keep me unfree,
I AM rising beyond every impurity,
with Purity's Light forever in me.**

4. Serapis Bey, help me see that I am not here to force people but to raise their insight, their knowledge, their vision so that they can voluntarily make certain changes.

Beloved Astrea, accelerate life
beyond all duality's struggle and strife,
consume all division between God and man,
accelerate fulfillment of God's perfect plan.

**Beloved Astrea, I lovingly call,
break down separation's invisible wall,
I surrender all lies causing the fall,
forever affirming the oneness of All.**

5. Serapis Bey, help me see if the fallen beings have forced me into reacting to them and against them.

O Elohim Peace, in Unity's Flame,
there is no more room for duality's game,
we know that all form is from the same source,
empowering us to plot a new course.

**O Elohim Peace, the bell now you ring,
causing all atoms to vibrate and sing,
I now see that there is no separate thing,
to my ego-based self I no longer cling.**

6. Serapis Bey, help me see and rise above any self-reinforcing spirals of reacting to or against people I meet in my family, workplace or elsewhere, so that I can break free from any karmic groups I may be involved with.

> O Elohim Peace, you help me to know,
> that Jesus has come your Flame to bestow,
> upon all who are ready to give up the strife,
> by following Christ into infinite life.

> **O Elohim Peace, through your eyes I see,**
> **that only in oneness will I ever be free,**
> **I give up the sense of a separate me,**
> **I AM crossing Samsara's turbulent sea.**

7. Serapis Bey, help me see and transcend the more subtle reactionary spirals, the sense that because the fallen beings have forced people into a downward spiral, I am justified in forcing people out of the downward spiral for their own good.

> O Elohim Peace, you show me the way,
> for clearing my mind from duality's fray,
> you pierce the illusions of both time and space,
> separation consumed by your Infinite Grace.

> **O Elohim Peace, what beauty your name,**
> **consuming within me duality's shame,**
> **It was through the vibration of your Golden Flame,**
> **that Christ the illusion of death overcame.**

8. Serapis Bey, help me see and transcend the subtle sense that I am here to give a service to earth and that the measure for evaluating whether I am successful in giving this service is that I see specific outer changes.

> O Elohim Peace, you bring now to Earth,
> the unstoppable flame of Cosmic Rebirth,
> I give up the sense that something is mine,
> allowing your Light through my being to shine.
>
> **O Elohim Peace, through your tranquility,**
> **we are free from the chaos of duality,**
> **in oneness with God a new identity,**
> **we are raising the Earth into Infinity.**

9. Serapis Bey, I now see that as long as I think my service on this planet depends on producing specific outer changes, that are tied to the free-will choices of other people, then I can never attain inner peace.

> Accelerate into Purity, I AM real,
> Accelerate into Purity, all life heal,
> Accelerate into Purity, I AM MORE,
> Accelerate into Purity, all will soar.
>
> Accelerate into Purity! (3X)
> Beloved Elohim Astrea.
> Accelerate into Purity! (3X)
> Beloved Gabriel and Hope.
> Accelerate into Purity! (3X)
> Beloved Serapis Bey.
> Accelerate into Purity! (3X)
> Beloved I AM.

## Part 2

1. Serapis Bey, help me see and transcend any conflict between my original love-based motivation for coming to earth, and the motivation and the view I have in my conscious mind and three higher bodies.

> Gabriel Archangel, your light I revere,
> immersed in your Presence, nothing I fear.
> A disciple of Christ, I do leave behind,
> the ego's desire for responding in kind.

**Gabriel Archangel, of this I am sure,
Gabriel Archangel, Christ light is the cure.
Gabriel Archangel, intentions so pure,
Gabriel Archangel, in you I'm secure.**

2. Serapis Bey, I see that I cannot be at peace with being in embodiment on earth, as long as I think I am here to produce specific changes, that are dependent on the free-will choices of other people. I see that my service to life does not depend on anything outside myself.

> Gabriel Archangel, I fear not the light,
> in purifications' fire, I delight.
> With your hand in mine, each challenge I face,
> I follow the spiral to infinite grace.

**Gabriel Archangel, of this I am sure,
Gabriel Archangel, Christ light is the cure.
Gabriel Archangel, intentions so pure,
Gabriel Archangel, in you I'm secure.**

3. Serapis Bey, I see that I give service by walking the path of self-mastery, and becoming an open door for the light from my I AM Presence, and from the hierarchy of ascended masters above me.

> Gabriel Archangel, your fire burning white,
> ascending with you, out of the night.
> My ego has nowhere to run and to hide,
> in ascension's bright spiral, with you I abide.
>
> **Gabriel Archangel, of this I am sure,**
> **Gabriel Archangel, Christ light is the cure.**
> **Gabriel Archangel, intentions so pure,**
> **Gabriel Archangel, in you I'm secure.**

4. Serapis Bey, help me see and transcend the many layers of deception from the fallen beings, aimed at preventing me from doing the one thing I came here to do, namely being an open door for the light.

> Gabriel Archangel, your trumpet I hear,
> announcing the birth of Christ drawing near.
> In lightness of being, I now am reborn,
> rising with Christ on bright Easter morn.
>
> **Gabriel Archangel, of this I am sure,**
> **Gabriel Archangel, Christ light is the cure.**
> **Gabriel Archangel, intentions so pure,**
> **Gabriel Archangel, in you I'm secure.**

5. Serapis Bey, help me see that I have the right to express my light because I have taken physical embodiment. My free will has become part of the equation on earth.

Uriel Archangel, immense is the power,
of angels of peace, all war to devour.
The demons of war, no match for your light,
consuming them all, with radiance so bright.

**Uriel Archangel, use your great sword,**
**Uriel Archangel, consume all discord,**
**Uriel Archangel, we're of one accord,**
**Uriel Archangel, we walk with the Lord.**

6. Serapis Bey, I now see that I have a right to be in embodiment, to be who I am and to be an open door for the light from the hierarchy above me. This is my God-given right.

Uriel Archangel, intense is the sound,
when millions of angels, their voices compound.
They build a crescendo, piercing the night,
life's glorious oneness revealed to our sight.

**Uriel Archangel, use your great sword,**
**Uriel Archangel, consume all discord,**
**Uriel Archangel, we're of one accord,**
**Uriel Archangel, we walk with the Lord.**

7. Serapis Bey, help me see and transcend the lie that expressing my light is something I cannot do until certain conditions are fulfilled. I see that there are no outer conditions that can prevent me from transcending myself and expressing more and more light.

Uriel Archangel, from out the Great Throne,
your millions of trumpets, sound the One Tone.
Consuming all discord with your harmony,
the sound of all sounds will set all life free.

**Uriel Archangel, use your great sword,**
**Uriel Archangel, consume all discord,**
**Uriel Archangel, we're of one accord,**
**Uriel Archangel, we walk with the Lord.**

8. Serapis Bey, help me see and transcend the perfectionism invented by the fallen beings in order to make me believe, that the expression of my light has to live up to some impossible standard.

Uriel Archangel, all war is now gone,
for you bring a message, from heart of the One.
The hearts of all men, now singing in peace,
the spirals of love, forever increase.

**Uriel Archangel, use your great sword,**
**Uriel Archangel, consume all discord,**
**Uriel Archangel, we're of one accord,**
**Uriel Archangel, we walk with the Lord.**

9. Serapis Bey, help me see and transcend the projections of the fallen beings that there is something wrong with my light and something wrong with me. Help me free myself from all desire to work towards having a state of perfection.

With angels I soar,
as I reach for MORE.
The angels so real,
their love all will heal.
The angels bring peace,
all conflicts will cease.
With angels of light,
we soar to new height.

**The rustling sound of angel wings,**
**what joy as even matter sings,**
**what joy as every atom rings,**
**in harmony with angel wings.**

## Part 3

1. Serapis Bey, help me see and transcend the tendency to use spiritual teachings and techniques to perfect the outer self, so that it lives up to the standard of the fallen beings.

Serapis Bey, what power lies,
behind your purifying eyes.
Serapis Bey, it is a treat,
to enter your sublime retreat.

**O Holy Spirit, flow through me,**
**I am the open door for thee.**
**O mighty rushing stream of Light,**
**transcendence is my sacred right.**

2. Serapis Bey, help me see that I will never become perfect because there is no state of perfection. The fallen beings will never accept the light no matter how it is expressed.

> Serapis Bey, what wisdom found,
> your words are always most profound.
> Serapis Bey, I tell you true,
> my mind has room for naught but you.

**O Holy Spirit, flow through me,
I am the open door for thee.
O mighty rushing stream of Light,
transcendence is my sacred right.**

3. Serapis Bey, help me see and transcend the lie that my light has to be accepted in order to do its work. I just need to express my light, and then let the light do its work. The success of my service does not depend on the reaction of other people.

> Serapis Bey, what love beyond,
> my heart does leap, as I respond.
> Serapis Bey, your life a poem,
> that calls me to my starry home.

**O Holy Spirit, flow through me,
I am the open door for thee.
O mighty rushing stream of Light,
transcendence is my sacred right.**

4. Serapis Bey, help me see that as long as I think my service depends upon the reaction of other people, I cannot be at peace. If I am not at peace, then I cannot be an open door for the Light.

Serapis Bey, your guidance sure,
my base is clear and white and pure.
Serapis Bey, no longer trapped,
by soul in which my self was wrapped.

**O Holy Spirit, flow through me,
I am the open door for thee.
O mighty rushing stream of Light,
transcendence is my sacred right.**

5. Serapis Bey, help me disconnect my idea of service from the desire to produce specific results or be acknowledged, recognized and validated by other people.

Serapis Bey, what healing balm,
in mind that is forever calm.
Serapis Bey, my thoughts are pure,
your discipline I shall endure.

**O Holy Spirit, flow through me,
I am the open door for thee.
O mighty rushing stream of Light,
transcendence is my sacred right.**

6. Serapis Bey, help me see and transcend the lack of self-worth, caused by my being rejected by the fallen beings. Help me overcome the tendency to compensate for that, by being validated by the fallen beings or anyone in this world.

Serapis Bey, what secret test,
for egos who want to be best.
Serapis Bey, expose in me,
all that is less than harmony.

## 15 | Invoking Peace in Service

> O Holy Spirit, flow through me,
> I am the open door for thee.
> O mighty rushing stream of Light,
> transcendence is my sacred right.

7. Serapis Bey, I see that I will never be perfect in the minds of the fallen beings. I will no more chase this carrot, I will stop being the donkey for the fallen beings, and instead be the open door for the light of the ascended masters.

> Serapis Bey, what moving sight,
> my self ascends to sacred height.
> Serapis Bey, forever free,
> in sacred synchronicity.

> O Holy Spirit, flow through me,
> I am the open door for thee.
> O mighty rushing stream of Light,
> transcendence is my sacred right.

8. Serapis Bey, help me see and transcend any ego-based motivation I have for walking the spiritual path. Help me see what my ego wants to get out of me walking the path.

> Serapis Bey, you balance all,
> the seven rays upon my call.
> Serapis Bey, in space and time,
> the pyramid of self, I climb.

> O Holy Spirit, flow through me,
> I am the open door for thee.
> O mighty rushing stream of Light,
> transcendence is my sacred right.

9. Serapis Bey, help me see and transcend any self-reinforcing spirals where I and other spiritual people reinforce an ego-based sense, that we are better than other people because we are following a specific guru or teaching.

> Serapis Bey, your Presence here,
> filling up my inner sphere.
> Life is now a sacred flow,
> God Purity I do bestow.

**O Holy Spirit, flow through me,
I am the open door for thee.
O mighty rushing stream of Light,
transcendence is my sacred right.**

## Part 4

1. Serapis Bey, I am willing to transcend the very patterns that take away my inner peace. I recognize consciously that I want inner peace, and I want to be successful in giving my service on this planet. I want to serve in peace and I want the peace of knowing that my service is successful.

> Master Nada, beauty's power,
> unfolding like a sacred flower.
> Master Nada, so sublime,
> a will that conquers even time.

**O Holy Spirit, flow through me,
I am the open door for thee.
O mighty rushing stream of Light,
transcendence is my sacred right.**

2. Serapis Bey, I do not resist you exposing the pattern in my mind that prevents me from having what I want. Help me see the mechanism and consciously let it go.

> Master Nada, you bestow,
> upon me wisdom's rushing flow.
> Master Nada, mind so strong
> rising on your wings of song.

**O Holy Spirit, flow through me,
I am the open door for thee.
O mighty rushing stream of Light,
transcendence is my sacred right.**

3. Serapis Bey, help me truly accept and acknowledge that I am special, I am unique. My uniqueness is not anchored in my four lower bodies, but in my I AM Presence and causal body.

> Master Nada, precious scent,
> your love is truly heaven-sent.
> Master Nada, kind and soft
> on wings of love we rise aloft.

**O Holy Spirit, flow through me,
I am the open door for thee.
O mighty rushing stream of Light,
transcendence is my sacred right.**

4. Serapis Bey, help me see and transcend the tendency to build an outer self that is special compared to other people. Help me recapture my sense of self-worth, by reconnecting to the fact that my specialness is in my God-given individuality, not in the individuality I have built as a reaction to the conditions created by the fallen beings.

> Master Nada, mother light,
> my heart is rising like a kite.
> Master Nada, from your view,
> all life is pure as morning dew.

> **O Holy Spirit, flow through me,**
> **I am the open door for thee.**
> **O mighty rushing stream of Light,**
> **transcendence is my sacred right.**

5. Serapis Bey, I now see that I do not need to gain the recognition of the fallen beings or other human beings because I have the recognition of my Creator and the ascended masters.

> Master Nada, truth you bring,
> as morning birds in love do sing.
> Master Nada, I now feel,
> your love that all four bodies heal.

> **O Holy Spirit, flow through me,**
> **I am the open door for thee.**
> **O mighty rushing stream of Light,**
> **transcendence is my sacred right.**

6. Serapis Bey, help me make a shift in my conscious mind that allows me to feel your recognition and validation of me. Help me experience your love for me that is constantly raining upon me from Above.

> Master Nada, serve in peace,
> as all emotions I release.
> Master Nada, life is fun,
> my solar plexus is a sun.

> **O Holy Spirit, flow through me,**
> **I am the open door for thee.**
> **O mighty rushing stream of Light,**
> **transcendence is my sacred right.**

7. Serapis Bey, I see that you are not the one who is limiting the light that streams to me. I am the one who does not recognize the light, because I have some limitation in my mind that makes me think I am not worthy of it or not capable of receiving it.

> Master Nada, love is free,
> with no conditions binding me.
> Master Nada, rise above,
> all human forms of lesser love.

> **O Holy Spirit, flow through me,**
> **I am the open door for thee.**
> **O mighty rushing stream of Light,**
> **transcendence is my sacred right.**

8. Serapis Bey, help me know at the level of my identity body that I am unique in an incomparable way. Help me bring it down towards my mental and emotional bodies, and then towards my conscious mind.

> Master Nada, balance all,
> the seven rays upon my call.
> Master Nada, rise and shine,
> your radiant beauty most divine.

**O Holy Spirit, flow through me,
I am the open door for thee.
O mighty rushing stream of Light,
transcendence is my sacred right.**

9. Serapis Bey, help me switch and experience your love. I am open to experiencing your love consciously. Help me make the shift right now so that I can live the rest of my life in peace, knowing that I am performing the greatest service I can perform by being who I am, by being an open door for the light that I am.

> Nada Dear, your Presence here,
> filling up my inner sphere.
> Life is now a sacred flow,
> God Peace on all I do bestow.

**O Holy Spirit, flow through me,
I am the open door for thee.
O mighty rushing stream of Light,
transcendence is my sacred right.**

## *Sealing:*

In the name of the Divine Mother, I fully accept that the power of these calls is used to set free the Ma-ter light, so it can outpicture the perfect vision of Christ for my own life, for all people and for the planet. In the name I AM THAT I AM, it is done! Amen.

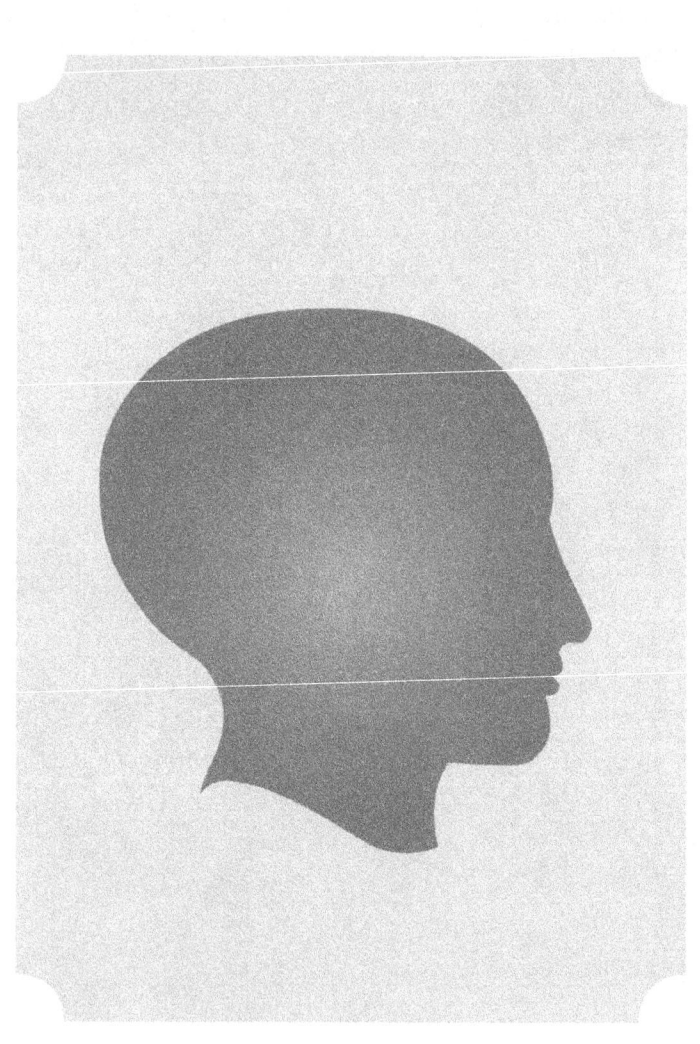

# 16 | FREEING YOUR INNER CREATIVITY

I am the Ascended Master Serapis Bey. We have now reached the seventh level where you encounter the combination of the Fourth Ray with the Seventh Ray of Freedom. The Seventh Ray of Freedom is in a sense both easy and the most difficult. It is easy in the sense that it puts no demands on you. It is difficult in the sense that it demands that you stop putting demands on yourself.

When students first come in contact with the ascended masters, they often have the idea that we are limiting their freedom in the sense that we are putting demands on you. Later, they may develop the idea that the fallen beings or the dark forces are limiting their freedom. In reality, there is only one thing limiting your freedom and that is what you do to yourself in your own mind. It is in the mind that you are imprisoned and it is in the mind that you need to manifest your freedom.

However, freedom is both something you manifest and something you cannot manifest, in the sense that

I have attempted to help you see that the problem on planet earth is that the fallen beings have induced people to use force. Therefore, you cannot overcome force by more force.

Certainly, the Seventh Ray is a ray that has a specific energy. You *can* and, of course, you *should,* invoke the energy of the Seventh Ray. You should not put yourself into a state of mind where you think that you have to use the energy of the Seventh Ray to beat down the opposition to your freedom. You will, of course, need to invoke the energies of the Seventh Ray to transform the perversions of the Seventh Ray. What limits your freedom is to some degree the energies from each of the seven rays that have been perverted through fear. You need to consume these by invoking the energies of each ray.

However, what truly limits your freedom is, of course, the energy, the beliefs and the ideas in your mind. These you cannot beat down by the Seventh Ray of Freedom. You can only come to see them for the unrealities they are and then simply walk away from them.

## The dramas that consume people's lives

When you look at planet earth, you will see that the vast majority of the people are wrapped up in – completely enveloped in, completely consumed by – some kind of drama. You see so many groups of people who have been fighting each other for generations, perhaps even for thousands of years. They are completely convinced that there is some reality to this drama and that they are working for God's cause and that those other people, whom they have been fighting, are working against Gods cause. You can see this in the Middle East between Jews, Christians and Muslims. You can see it in many other places in the world. It is clear that when you are caught up in such a drama, you are taking yourself very seriously, you are taking your cause very seriously. If you are taking every aspect of life, every little detail of life, so seriously, you cannot be free. You are, so to speak, wrapped up in yourself. Think about this popular saying of how so many people are wrapped up in themselves. There is so much internal conflict and struggle that all of their energy and attention is simply consumed by this. Well, what I want to point out to you is that it is very common that when people find ascended master teachings, they use the teachings to overcome some of the struggles you see in the world.

In many cases, the egos of the students succeed in having the students create another drama, which is where you use the spiritual path – and often the dark forces or even other people that you meet on the spiritual path – to create another drama. You, of course, do not see it as a drama. Then again, all of the people in the world who are consumed by dramas do not see it as a drama either; they see it as reality. You also come to see it as reality that you are battling the dark forces or that you are in some kind of disagreement with other students you meet on the spiritual path, perhaps in a spiritual organization.

The trick of the ego, the trick of the fallen beings, is to make you think that there is a real problem that you need to solve. Therefore, you cannot be free until the problem is solved. Of course, the problem requires that some changes must happen in the world. In most cases, this means that other people need to change so that you can solve the problem and be free.

As I have said before, you will never be free if you think your freedom depends on the free-will choices of other people. You can, however, be free by recognizing that your freedom depends only on your own free-will choices and that you have the power, right now, to free yourself from all of the internal beliefs and mechanisms that make you think you have to react to other people, you have to do something in the world. You can never be free if you take the spiritual path so seriously and if you are completely wrapped up in walking your own path and battling whatever you are battling. Even battling the ego can become a drama, and, of course, you cannot overcome the ego by using the ego. You will not overcome the ego through a drama created by the ego, and that is the danger of giving any kind of spiritual teaching.

## The dream of an ultimate state

As I inspired this messenger to realize recently, there are people in the world who claim to be enlightened. If you claim that you are enlightened, then you are in a sense saying, at least in the minds of most people, that you have reached some ultimate state. You may gather followers who are not willing to take responsibility for themselves and are therefore looking for a guru with some absolute state of consciousness. The guru and the students may create a self-reinforcing spiral.

The problem is that if you think you have reached an ultimate state on earth, you will not go any further. That means you will be denying the aspect of the ego that you still have. I know some people will say that if you are enlightened, you have no ego left and that is true. But then you are no longer in embodiment on earth because you cannot remain in embodiment unless you have some aspect of ego left. It may be very slight and you may have reached a high level of consciousness. If you think there is nothing beyond your state of consciousness, you can only think so by denying the element of ego you have left. Then, you cannot let go of that ego and be free to ascend.

## 16 | Freeing Your Inner Creativity

### Creativity is the antidote to control

The ascension is a process that requires you to be completely free. The process of self-mastery is also a process that requires you to attain a very high degree of freedom. Not in the same way as you have when you ascend, but in the way that you are free to express your creative abilities. What does it mean to be free, to be creative? It means to understand what the fallen beings have done in order to shut down creativity and make you limit your creativity.

Do you understand, my beloved, that the fallen beings are attempting to control everything on earth? How do you control? You must shut down creativity because what is the nature of creativity? It is unpredictable, it is spontaneous. It comes up with something new, perhaps even something so new that nobody could even imagine it.

The fallen beings are mortally afraid of your creativity. They also know that nothing in this world can limit creativity. The entire nature of creativity is that it transcends boundaries. There are no boundaries that can truly limit your creativity, except the boundaries created in your own mind so you do not dare to even express it.

The primary means used by the fallen beings to shut down people's creativity is to create the idea that there is a standard against which everything must be measured. The standard has only two polarities. Either something is good enough, perfect, acceptable, or it is a mistake, bad, unacceptable. This evaluation, this judgment, has nothing to do with creativity. It is, we might say, the antithesis of creativity.

When you first came to this planet, you came to express your light, your creativity, your individuality. The fallen beings did everything they could to make you feel rejected, to make you feel that there was something wrong with your light. Your creativity was not good enough, *you* were not good enough.

This caused so many people to go into this race that I have talked about of trying to be perfect, trying to live up to the standard, thinking that if only you are good enough, then you will be accepted. You understand, my beloved, that if you have a mechanism in your mind that seeks to compare your expression to an outer standard before you dare to express yourself, then, right there, you have shut down your creativity.

Creativity is spontaneous! You have become so used to evaluating everything with the linear, analytical mind. The fallen beings have induced in most people this very subtle idea that everything should be analyzed. Everything should be evaluated by the analytical mind, which compares everything to a standard. Most people are not aware of the standard they are using. Sometimes they are aware of a standard put upon them by society. Certainly, the educational systems of the world are all geared towards making you accept that there is a standard and your creativity needs to be compared to it. Even the educational institutions that teach some form of creative expression, be it art or whatever, are still reinforcing this idea that creativity must be compared to a standard.

## Creativity knows no standards

Creativity is about going beyond the standards. How did anything on earth evolve, how did it grow to a higher level? Only by going beyond the existing level. Do you not see that there is a creative process built into nature? This is what I call the primary laws of nature that ensure constant growth, constant transcendence. The fallen beings have created the secondary laws of nature in an attempt to shut down this transcendence.

They want to stop the growth, stop the clock, set everything at a certain level from which it cannot transcend. They want to do this because they want control, and you cannot control something unless you can predict it. You cannot predict it as long as it is in an upward spiral instead of going around in a circle. The fallen beings know they cannot stop movement; they have realized this much. They are trying to make it circular instead of an ascending spiral.

There is movement and there are certain cycles. If they are going around in a circle, they can at least predict them. They know what is coming up just as you see in the progressions of the seasons, where you know when to plant and you know when to harvest because it is always the same, even though it cannot always be predicted down to the minute.

Because of the built-in process of creativity, the fallen beings have never been successful. They have in the past created civilizations that were locked in a certain pattern for a long time. They have also created some civilizations that became so locked in a certain pattern that they eventually went into a downward spiral and therefore declined or even collapsed.

This is what I have said is the force built into the Mother and that we have sometimes called the force behind the second law of thermodynamics. A closed system must self-destruct in order for the upward progression to resume. Why is there even allowed to be a closed system? Because of free will and because you are allowed to have the experience for a time that you have established this society that does not change and therefore supposedly could never disappear but will last forever, or at least for a thousand years as many have dreamed about.

The fallen beings want to create a society where no one dares to express creativity, true creativity. Instead, they think creativity means working within the boundaries defined by the leaders of that society, meaning the fallen beings. What we of the Chohans aim to take you through is, of course, a process where you free your intention, your imagination, your creative abilities so that you dare to express, not the kind of creativity defined by the world, but the true creativity coming from your I AM Presence.

## *How your I AM Presence looks at life*

Your I AM Presence looks at life in a completely different way than you do with your outer mind. This is not said to blame you. It can be no other way when you are in embodiment. You can still begin to glimpse and certainly understand that your I AM Presence has a different view. Therefore, the I AM Presence has a different purpose.

The I AM Presence wants you – when you are a spiritual student and you are deliberately engaging in the upward path, the spiritual path – to transcend yourself so that you reach your ascension point as quickly as possible. It also wants you to fulfill your Divine plan in this lifetime. What is that going to require? It is not going to require that you conform to the standards of your society, your family or your workplace. It is going to require that you are daring to do something different.

Look at how many spiritual students have led lives that were not rational or practical or the way their parents or society wanted them to live their lives. Look how many times that people have changed jobs, taken time off to go to a spiritual retreat, changed partners, done this and done that. You may have done things that seem to be irrational but it is because there is something driving you. You realize you have to fit a lot of experiences into one lifetime, and therefore you cannot work in the same job or necessarily have the same partner for an entire lifetime. You need to move around and look at life from different perspectives in order to resolve the issues in your own mind that are standing in the way of your ascension or your growth.

There is no need to look at your life with this judgmental attitude of worrying about what mistakes you have made. My beloved, if you desire to look at your life and evaluate what mistakes you have made, then that is, of course, your right. Then, I have to say: "I, Serapis Bey, the Chohan of the Fourth Ray cannot help you there." There are many students who come to my retreat and they have this desire. They want to have me sit down and look at their life with them and tell them where they made a mistake, what they did wrong, what they should have done better. I must tell them that I cannot help them with this. Some become angry, some become disappointed, some leave. What I tell you is this: "I cannot help you determine where you made a mistake. I can help you look at your life and see that everything you did was an experiment."

There are no mistakes in experimentation, my beloved. You may have a goal for your experiment and you may say: "My goal did not come to pass." For example, when Thomas Edison wanted to invent the light bulb, he tried many materials that did not work. Were they mistakes? Did he blame himself for using the "wrong" material? No, he simply kept experimenting until he found one that worked and that is how I can help you look at your life.

I can also help you go further and see that in many cases you did something in your life and you had a conscious intention of how things should go. That conscious intention was not fulfilled. Therefore, you were hurt or disappointed, or you started blaming yourself for having done wrong and made a terrible mistake. What I can help you step back and see is that your I AM Presence does not look at that event the way you look at it.

## A higher goal than conscious intentions

You see, my beloved, it is inevitable on a planet like this that you come to formulate certain conscious intentions that are not in accordance with your Divine plan or your highest potential for growth. This does not mean that they were wrong. It does mean that the purpose of doing something was not actually to fulfill the conscious goal that you had.

The purpose of doing something from the perspective of your I AM presence was that you did it enough until you realized: "I do not want to do this anymore." Then you start thinking: "Was it my intent that was the problem, not the outer result or the lack of it?" What I can help you see is that in many cases, where you have been disappointed in life or made what you think is a mistake, the real issue here is that you need to step back and say: "But why did I strive to do this? Why did I have this goal? Why did I think that there was only this particular way to live? Why did I think I had to play this game that my society has conditioned me to play?"

There are certain people who can only learn through the School of Hard Knocks. There are certain things that all of us only learn by, so to speak, going into the School of Hard Knocks. It is fine to say that we have a spiritual teacher and that we are in a protected environment where we are always in contact with a spiritual teacher who can help us evaluate everything. But there are certain elements of the process where we simply need to go out and experiment ourselves. We need to – to put it bluntly – pound our heads against a rock wall a sufficient number of times until we realize that pounding your head against the wall is not going to break down the wall. Therefore, you need to re-evaluate what you are doing and why you are doing it. This is simply part of growing in the material world especially, of course, in its current condition where it has the secondary laws of nature.

## Why separate beings cannot be free

My beloved, I have talked about the secondary laws of nature without defining them. Let me give you a little more of an impression of how they work. If you go to a pure environment where there are no secondary laws of nature, you will see that in such an environment (which we have called the Garden of Eden or Maitreya's Mystery School) you are free to express your creativity. This does not mean that you are always going to create a result that is really what you intended or that is really what you want to live with for a time.

What happens in a pure environment is that anything you can create, you can uncreate instantly. The reason this is possible is that you also have an instant return of whatever you create, you have an instant manifestation of what you create. If you are sending out what you today would call an aggressive intent against another person, it will come back to you right away. In an environment like that, you cannot have certain experiences because there would be an instant return and you would instantly feel the pain. You could not go into separation in such an environment and start acting like an independent being who can do whatever they want regardless of how it affects the whole.

In a pure environment you can do whatever you want, but you will instantly experience how it affects the whole because it will be reflected back to you. The only way to avoid this is to have an environment where there is a delay factor. You are not getting an instant return on what you are sending out, and this means you can, for a time, have the illusion in your mind that you are a separate being and you can get away with certain things.

The entire outlook on life of the fallen beings is that they have a desire to experience that they can get away with things. They can separate themselves from God, they can create their own world, they can define the rules. All of us need to have some experience with this. We have all needed to experience this separation for a time.

You do understand that when you go into separation, you are not free; you cannot be free. It is, per definition, impossible to be both a separate being and be free because being in separation can only happen by defining certain limitations and boundaries and those will limit you.

You may not experience it in the beginning. You may actually think that by rebelling against God, as the fallen beings claim, you gain your freedom. You will see that there are teachings on the planet that claim that when you are following God's will, you are in a straitjacket and it is only by rebelling that you claim your freedom. This is what some satanic ideas and satanic teachings will say.

That is how it feels in the beginning because there is the delay factor where you are not having the instant return of what you are sending out. That delay factor cannot last forever, and there will come a point where now you are beginning to feel unfree.

Let me just ask you this, my beloved, as an intellectual, logical exercise. The fallen beings will, on the one hand, claim that you are only free by rebelling against God. At the same time, they are defining God as the enemy who is limiting you. Well, why do they need to define God this way? Why couldn't they simply walk away from God and say: "God is irrelevant to us, we are doing whatever we want." It is because when you go into duality, you cannot do whatever you want. You *must* have an opponent. The fallen beings have turned God into their opponent, or each other into opponents or other beings, other human beings, into opponents. You must have something to fight against, otherwise you cannot uphold the illusion that you are a separate being. Having something to fight against takes your freedom away. It can be no other way. In order to be free, again, to express your creativity, you need to dismantle these mechanisms, these beliefs of what you think you should be doing in life.

## Defining the secondary laws of nature

To return to the secondary laws of nature, the Law of Free Will allows you to go into this separate space and it allows you to define certain laws in there. What the fallen beings have done is that they have defined certain laws that have caused matter to become more dense. The matter in the universe in which you live is more dense than it originally was. I should say that it is not more dense all over the universe, but certainly on planet earth matter is more dense than when the planet was originally created by the Elohim.

This has several effects, first of all it hides that there is a spiritual realm. You cannot see this with your physical senses and the outer mind. It also hides the idea that things are coming back to you. You think that you can build some kind of wall out of matter that will protect you from the return of what we have called your karma. The fallen beings are attempting to do this, and you can delay things but you cannot delay them forever.

There does come a point where your karma comes back to you and there is nothing you can do about it. In creating the secondary laws of nature and making things more dense, you are also making it more difficult to change things. When it does become apparent that things did not work out the way you thought they were going to work out, and that you could not forever escape your karma, then it becomes very difficult to extricate yourself from it.

This has had the effect of creating a learning environment that is extremely unforgiving compared to the environment you had in the Garden of Eden with Maitreya. In the original pure environment you can create something that you don't particularly like and that is unpleasant when it comes back to you, but you can instantly uncreate it. In the present environment you have a delay factor against what is coming back. You can send something out and it does not come back to you instantly. When it *does* come back to you, then it is also much more difficult to undo it.

You also have a situation where, because of the density of matter, matter itself is very, very unforgiving. You can instantly create consequences that do hit you instantly and that will affect you for a long time to come. You know very well that if you step out from a tall building, you will fall down and there is nothing you can do about that. There are many other choices in life where you have a very instant unpleasant effect. Or you have an effect that will last for the rest of that lifetime from just one choice. This was not there in the original learning environment.

Do you see that the world in which you have grown up has conditioned you to think that the main concern you have for anything you do in life should be to avoid these very difficult and unpleasant consequences of your actions? Can you see that if your focus is on avoiding making a mistake, avoiding doing something wrong, avoiding creating a very unpleasant consequence, then you are not actually being creative? Creativity is not a reaction to or against conditions on earth. Creativity is not you relating to the material world and current conditions. Creativity is you relating to your I AM Presence and allowing the individuality and the creativity of the Presence to be expressed through you in the material world.

You see that it is not a matter of indefinitely trying to avoid negative consequences. It is actually a matter of being creative so that you either transcend or change the conditions that are creating these negative consequences. This is how the world progresses.

## A new definition of genius

There have been people who have been tuned in to this creative flow. You may see certain people who have been called geniuses because they could come up with an idea that nobody else had thought about. Many people were only able to do this once in a lifetime or maybe a few times. They were only able to do it in a specific area, but many times they could not transfer that to their own lives. You will see that many of these so-called geniuses, such as Einstein, were also eccentric and had what you might call limited success in their personal lives. There was a disconnect between their chosen field of study and everyday life.

Well, my beloved, we would rather see you become geniuses in everyday life, even though we also would like to see you be geniuses in some area where you have the potential to express something new. The purpose of the course of self-mastery is to have you be a genius in your everyday life by being creative and learning how to use your in-built, Divine, spiritual creativity to create the life and the life experience you desire in this lifetime so that it can facilitate your growth.

It may not be your goal to make your ascension in this lifetime, but it certainly will be in your Divine plan to make considerable progress towards the ascension. Many of you do have it in your Divine plan to qualify for your ascension by the end of this lifetime. This does require sometimes that you do some things that from the perspective of other people in your environment can seem very irrational, very irresponsible, very strange.

## Ego as a buffer between you and the world

This is creativity in the sense that it transcends the boundaries you have in your consciousness, the limitations that are holding you back. What is creativity for you? Well, I cannot say, my beloved. I cannot say because you cannot know with your outer mind what is creativity.

You understand what I am saying here? What have the fallen beings done? They have created a mechanism in your mind that is between you and the world. What is ego, my beloved? It is a reaction to you being rejected in this world. Therefore, you are trying to create a mechanism that protects you from the material world and the conditions here. It is a buffer zone between you and the world. Part of this is that you are evaluating everything you do before you do it. You are concerned about the potential consequences.

Will this kill me instantly? Will it cripple me so that I have to sit in a wheelchair for the rest of my life? Also more subtle evaluations, such as what will other people say or think about me? What are the norms of my society for how I should behave and should not behave? You are used to evaluating everything before you express it, but this is not creativity. Creativity is that you connect, the Conscious You connects, intuitively to your

I AM Presence. You are not evaluating with your outer mind what the Presence is going to do through you in order to stop this, if the Presence wants to do something that you are not in agreement with or that might embarrass you.

## Letting the Presence work through you

You will not know with the outer mind what your Presence wants to do. You understand this? The moment you make an intuitive connection with your I AM Presence and then go into the analytical mind, at that moment you have shut off the creative flow. Your I AM Presence must step back, respect your free will and simply not express itself through you.

When you are evaluating with the outer mind, you are shutting down the creative flow from your Presence. The only way to know what the Presence is going to do through you is to experience it as it is happening. You cannot know ahead of time, and then, if you approve, allow your Presence to express it. You will need to let the Presence express what it wants to express and experience it only as it is happening.

If you are not willing to do this, if you are not willing to be spontaneous, you are not truly creative. It cannot be any other way. You cannot circumvent this. Therefore, we might call it a law. You cannot be connected to your Presence and at the same time be evaluating what the Presence should express. You cannot connect to your Presence through the analytical mind.

You can, of course, realize that your Presence is not going to do something that is going to kill you. It is not going to want to express something through you that is going to lock you even more in a limited state. The Presence wants to set you free from limitations.

So many people are afraid of their own creativity because they too have come to believe that the only way to avoid bad consequences is to control everything. They think that the ego is right when it wants to control everything and make everything predictable. You become afraid of being spontaneous; you become afraid of what is unpredictable.

Why did Jesus say that unless you become as a little child, you cannot enter the kingdom? It is because the kingdom of God is a state of consciousness, the Christ consciousness. The Christ consciousness is when you are connected to your I AM Presence and the I AM Presence can express itself through you. As Jesus said, I can of my own self do nothing; it is the father, meaning the I AM Presence, within me who is doing the work. This is Christhood.

## Creativity must be expressed

Christhood may be a little bit above the 96th level, but self-mastery means that you unlock your creativity and allow it to flow through you. This you need to start doing before you can move from my retreat to the retreat of Hilarion on the Fifth Ray. I have said that the Fourth Ray is sort of at a nexus between the first three rays and the last three. The last three rays is where you need to begin to express your creativity.

It is not just a matter of learning more and more as you go through this course. You have been going through a normal sort of progression in the first three rays, and I am here to take you to a point where you are ready to go to the last three where it is not a matter of learning. It is a matter of expressing. It is not a matter of you sitting in your ivory tower learning something about yourself. It is a matter of daring to actually express the creativity of the seven rays and using that creativity to change your life and your life experience. How will you unlock the creativity? Well, at the etheric level of my retreat we both teach you, as I have taught you now. We give you ideas, we challenge your view of the world, but we also take you through a number of exercises that are aimed at helping you unlock that creativity and daring to be spontaneous. You can, of course, help yourself tremendously by also doing something at the conscious level.

Your life will not change until you bring what you learn at the retreat down through the identity, mental, emotional body and finally into the physical. I encourage you to engage in some kind of activity that is spontaneous. I will leave the choice up to you because there are many such activities. It can be painting, drawing, dance, music—anything you desire.

## A program for unlocking creativity

What I would like to suggest, though, is that you build a daily program of studying this dictation and giving the invocation based on it. You take some time afterwards to sit quietly. What you do is to have a notepad and a pen and then you take some moments to tune in to your I AM Presence. When I say tune in, I do not mean that you do this with the analytical mind. I do not mean that you sit there and create a ritual in your mind and that you think about how it is to tune in to your Presence. I ask you to, as much as you can, calm the mind, quiet the mind and then tune in. Then, write whatever comes to you without evaluating at all what is coming.

It may be that what is coming to you is actually something that is expressed from your subconscious mind. It may be that there are certain things you need to see in your subconscious mind and therefore that is what is coming to your attention.

These maybe things that are blocking you from attuning to your I AM Presence. You can, by reading this, evaluate it. You can use what comes up when you give the invocation for this chapter or you can give other invocations and decrees as is appropriate. For example, if you have a certain fear, you might make calls to Archangel Michael. If you have a certain tie to something dark, something unpleasant, you can give calls to the Elohim Astrea to cut you free. There are calls, there are decrees and invocations, for every master, for every issue that could come up (See *www.transcendencetoolbox.com*).

It might also be that something comes to you that you had not dared to think about. There may be something about how to change your outer situation that you have not dared to think about with your conscious mind. Then you need to sit down and evaluate. Will you make that change or will you not? I am not saying that you should necessarily make every change that comes to you. It may just be that you need to see something so you can make a conscious choice as to whether you change or do not change.

Again, keep in mind that you have done things that were done for the purpose of seeing that you do not want to do this anymore. It can be the same when you get something from within. There are many spiritual students who have thought that anytime they get something from within, it must be from their I AM Presence or the ascended masters, but this is not always the case. It can be from a certain aspect of your ego, and it can be that this is coming up because you need to come to the point where you consciously see that this is not a higher direction, this is not something coming from a higher source. Therefore, by consciously recognizing this, you can expose an aspect of your ego and then you can increase your attunement with your I AM Presence and get real directions from above. I earlier said that if you think you are enlightened, there are certain aspects of the ego you must deny and therefore you are trapped. There are also spiritual students who have become trapped because they think they receive a certain divine direction or higher inspiration but it is not higher in the sense that it comes from the I AM Presence. It may come from beings in the mental or the identity realm. It may come from your identity body or your mental body but it is not coming from the Presence and the ascended masters. There may be times where there are students who get these persistent directions that they think are valid, and the purpose of it is to come to the point where you realize that this is not the highest, there is something higher.

## Why the path seems complicated

Yes my beloved, this is confusing, this is complicated. Do you know why it seems complicated? What did I say in the beginning? Freedom is freedom from the mechanisms in your own mind. This is where you win freedom: in your own mind. Do you not understand that when you are looking from inside your own mind, it is difficult to see the mechanisms you have created? Why? Because you created these mechanisms to give yourself the illusion that you are a separate being.

If you could see that you are not really a separate being – that this is just an illusion – then it would no longer give you the sense of reality. You may have been in a theatre where you see the sets on the stage. You may have had the experience of going behind the sets and seeing that it is just an impression that only works when you are looking at it from the theatre. As soon as you go behind, you see that it is all fake. Well that is how it is in your mind. When you are sitting in the theatre and looking at the stage, it all seems real. If you go behind the stage, it is, of course, all fake. When you are sitting there in your own mind, it seems so confusing, so difficult to see, so complicated. You are thinking: "Oh, but how can I ever be free of this? How will I ever see through it?"

My beloved, I completely understand the feeling because I had it myself before I won my ascension, and I am capable of remembering how it was before I ascended. I also know that by taking one step at a time, you are thinning the veil and there will come points when the clouds will part and you see a ray of the sun of your I AM Presence.

## Conclusion

I have taken you through seven steps in this book. If you follow them diligently, you will make progress and one day you will be ready to follow the initiations under my beloved brother Hilarion, who will teach you how to follow the old axiom: "Physician, heal thyself!"

It has been my great joy to tutor you at my retreat. It has been my great joy to bring forth these dictations that can stimulate your outer mind. I am grateful for the opportunity to make this material physical where anyone can read it and therefore have the opportunity to decide: "Will I just read it or will I perform the exercises? Will I do this mechanically or will I begin to do it creatively? Will I do it as an outer exercise or will I really tune in to the Presence of Serapis Bey?"

The entire purpose, in a sense, of these seven levels of initiation is to help you consciously tune in to the Presence that I AM. If you could experience my Presence with your outer mind, it would anchor the growth you have gone through at the etheric level in your physical life and outer mind in a way that you may not be able to even imagine before you experience my Presence.

Therefore, I do hope that there will come a point where the clouds will part and you will see me as I AM. For I am the ascended master Serapis Bey, Chohan of the Fourth Ray and:

I AM free

in pur-i-ty.

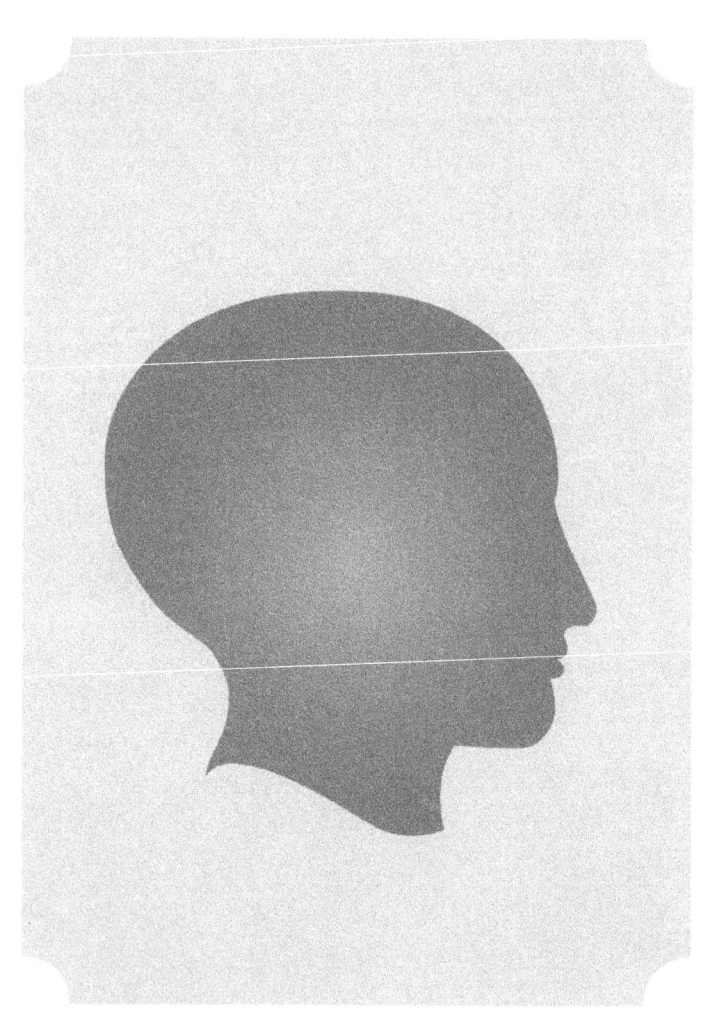

# 17 | INVOKING FREEDOM TO CREATE

In the name I AM THAT I AM, Jesus Christ, I call to my I AM Presence to flow through the I Will Be Presence that I AM and give this invocation with full power. I call to beloved Elohim Purity and Astrea and Arcturus and Victoria, Archangel Gabriel and Hope and Zadkiel and Amethyst, Serapis Bey and Saint Germain to help me transcend all mechanisms in my mind that block the creative flow from my I AM Presence. Help me see and surrender all patterns that block my oneness with Serapis Bey and with my I AM Presence, including …

[Make personal calls]

## Part 1

1. Serapis Bey, help me see how I am limiting my freedom and what I do to myself in my own mind. Help

me overcome the illusion that I have to use the energy of the Seventh Ray to beat down the opposition to my freedom.

> Beloved Astrea, your heart is so true,
> your Circle and Sword of white and blue,
> cut all life free from dramas unwise,
> on wings of Purity our planet will rise.

**Beloved Astrea, in God Purity,
accelerate all of my life energy,
raising my mind into true unity
with the Masters of love in Infinity.**

2. Serapis Bey, help me see the beliefs and ideas in my mind, help me see them for the unrealities they are and then simply walk away from them. Help me see where I am taking myself and life too seriously.

> Beloved Astrea, from Purity's Ray,
> send forth deliverance to all life today,
> acceleration to Purity, I AM now free
> from all that is less than love's Purity.

**Beloved Astrea, in oneness with you,
your circle and sword of electric blue,
with Purity's Light cutting right through,
raising within me all that is true.**

3. Serapis Bey, help me see any internal conflicts and struggles that consume my energy and attention. Help me see if I have used the teachings of the ascended masters to create a drama of battling dark forces or other students I meet in a spiritual organization.

> Beloved Astrea, accelerate us all,
> as for your deliverance I fervently call,
> set all life free from vision impure
> beyond fear and doubt, I AM rising for sure.
>
> **Beloved Astrea, I AM willing to see,**
> **all of the lies that keep me unfree,**
> **I AM rising beyond every impurity,**
> **with Purity's Light forever in me.**

4. Serapis Bey, help me transcend the trick of the ego, the trick of the fallen beings, of making me think there is a real problem that I need to solve and that I cannot be free until the problem is solved.

> Beloved Astrea, accelerate life
> beyond all duality's struggle and strife,
> consume all division between God and man,
> accelerate fulfillment of God's perfect plan.
>
> **Beloved Astrea, I lovingly call,**
> **break down separation's invisible wall,**
> **I surrender all lies causing the fall,**
> **forever affirming the oneness of All.**

5. Serapis Bey, I see that I will never be free as long as I think my freedom depends on the free-will choices of other people. My freedom depends only on my own free-will choices, and I have the power to free myself from the internal beliefs and mechanisms that make me think I have to react to other people or do something in the world.

Beloved Arcturus, release now the flow,
of Violet Flame to help all life grow,
in ever-expanding circles of Light,
it pulses within every atom so bright.

**Beloved Arcturus, thou Elohim Free,
I open my heart to your reality,
expanding my heart into Infinity,
your flame is the key to my God-victory.**

6. Serapis Bey, help me see that even battling the ego can become a drama, and that I cannot overcome the ego by using the ego. I will not overcome the ego through a drama created by the ego.

Beloved Arcturus, be with me alway,
reborn, I am ready to face a new day,
I have no attachments to life here on Earth,
I claim a new life in your Flame of Rebirth.

**Beloved Arcturus, your Violet Flame pure,
is for every ailment the ultimate cure,
against it no darkness could ever endure,
my freedom it will forever ensure.**

7. Serapis Bey, I see that the nature of creativity is that it transcends boundaries. There are no boundaries that can limit my creativity, except the boundaries created in my own mind so I do not dare to even express it.

## 17 | Invoking Freedom to Create

Beloved Arcturus, your bright violet fire,
now fills every atom, raising them higher,
the space in each atom all filled with your light,
as matter itself is shining so bright.

**Beloved Arcturus, your transforming Grace,
empowers me now every challenge to face,
as your violet light floods my inner space,
towards my ascension I willingly race.**

8. Serapis Bey, help me transcend the lie of the fallen beings that there is a standard against which everything must be measured. I see that the dualistic judgment has nothing to do with creativity. It is the antithesis of creativity.

Beloved Arcturus, bring in a new age,
help Earth and humanity turn a new page,
your transforming light gives me certainty,
Saint Germain's Golden Age is a reality.

**Beloved Arcturus, I surrender all fear,
I AM feeling your Presence so tangibly near,
with your Freedom's Song filling my ear,
I know that to God I AM ever so dear.**

9. Serapis Bey, help me walk away from the race of trying to be perfect, trying to live up to the standard, thinking that if only I am good enough, then I will be accepted.

Accelerate into Purity, I AM real,
Accelerate into Purity, all life heal,
Accelerate into Purity, I AM MORE,
Accelerate into Purity, all will soar.

Accelerate into Purity! (3X)
Beloved Elohim Astrea.
Accelerate into Purity! (3X)
Beloved Gabriel and Hope.
Accelerate into Purity! (3X)
Beloved Serapis Bey.
Accelerate into Purity! (3X)
Beloved I AM.

## Part 2

1. Serapis Bey, help me see that if I have a mechanism in my mind that seeks to compare my expression to an outer standard before I dare to express myself, then I have shut down my creativity.

> Gabriel Archangel, your light I revere,
> immersed in your Presence, nothing I fear.
> A disciple of Christ, I do leave behind,
> the ego's desire for responding in kind.
>
> **Gabriel Archangel, of this I am sure,**
> **Gabriel Archangel, Christ light is the cure.**
> **Gabriel Archangel, intentions so pure,**
> **Gabriel Archangel, in you I'm secure.**

2. Serapis Bey, help me overcome the subtle illusion that everything should be analyzed and evaluated by the analytical mind. Help me transcend the standards put upon me by society and the educational systems of the world.

## 17 | Invoking Freedom to Create

> Gabriel Archangel, I fear not the light,
> in purifications' fire, I delight.
> With your hand in mine, each challenge I face,
> I follow the spiral to infinite grace.
>
> **Gabriel Archangel, of this I am sure,**
> **Gabriel Archangel, Christ light is the cure.**
> **Gabriel Archangel, intentions so pure,**
> **Gabriel Archangel, in you I'm secure.**

3. Serapis Bey, help me see that I cannot reach my ascension point or fulfill my Divine plan by conforming to the standards of my society, family or workplace. I need to dare to do something different.

> Gabriel Archangel, your fire burning white,
> ascending with you, out of the night.
> My ego has nowhere to run and to hide,
> in ascension's bright spiral, with you I abide.
>
> **Gabriel Archangel, of this I am sure,**
> **Gabriel Archangel, Christ light is the cure.**
> **Gabriel Archangel, intentions so pure,**
> **Gabriel Archangel, in you I'm secure.**

4. Serapis Bey, help me overcome the tendency to look at my life with this judgmental attitude of worrying about what mistakes I have made. Help me look at my life and see that everything I did was an experiment and that there are no mistakes in experimentation.

Gabriel Archangel, your trumpet I hear,
announcing the birth of Christ drawing near.
In lightness of being, I now am reborn,
rising with Christ on bright Easter morn.

**Gabriel Archangel, of this I am sure,**
**Gabriel Archangel, Christ light is the cure.**
**Gabriel Archangel, intentions so pure,**
**Gabriel Archangel, in you I'm secure.**

5. Serapis Bey, help me see that in many cases my conscious intention was not fulfilled, but this does not mean it was a mistake. Help me step back and see that my I AM Presence does not look at an event the way I look at it.

Zadkiel Archangel, your flow is so swift,
in your violet light, I instantly shift,
into a vibration in which I am free,
from all limitations of the lesser me.

**Zadkiel Archangel, encircle the earth,**
**Zadkiel Archangel, with your violet girth,**
**Zadkiel Archangel, unstoppable mirth,**
**Zadkiel Archangel, our planet's rebirth.**

6. Serapis Bey, help me see that in many cases my conscious intentions were not in accordance with my Divine plan or my highest potential for growth. Therefore, the purpose of doing something was not to fulfill my conscious goal, but to realize that I do not want to do this anymore.

Zadkiel Archangel, I truly aspire,
to being the master of your violet fire.
Wielding the power, of your alchemy,
I use Sacred Word, to set all life free.

**Zadkiel Archangel, encircle the earth,**
**Zadkiel Archangel, with your violet girth,**
**Zadkiel Archangel, unstoppable mirth,**
**Zadkiel Archangel, our planet's rebirth.**

7. Serapis Bey, help me see that in many cases, where I have been disappointed or made a mistake, the real issue was that I needed to become aware of what I really want in life.

Zadkiel Archangel, your violet light,
transforming the earth, with unstoppable might.
So swiftly our planet, beginning to spin,
with legions of angels, our victory we win.

**Zadkiel Archangel, encircle the earth,**
**Zadkiel Archangel, with your violet girth,**
**Zadkiel Archangel, unstoppable mirth,**
**Zadkiel Archangel, our planet's rebirth.**

8. Serapis Bey, help me overcome my desires for going into separation and duality. Help me become free to express my creativity by dismantling the mechanisms and beliefs of what I think I should be doing in life.

Zadkiel Archangel, your violet flame,
the earth and humanity, never the same.
Saint Germain's Golden Age, is a reality,
what glorious wonder, I joyously see.

**Zadkiel Archangel, encircle the earth,
Zadkiel Archangel, with your violet girth,
Zadkiel Archangel, unstoppable mirth,
Zadkiel Archangel, our planet's rebirth.**

9. Serapis Bey, help me overcome the conditioning that the main concern for anything I do in life should be to avoid these very difficult and unpleasant consequences of my actions.

With angels I soar,
as I reach for MORE.
The angels so real,
their love all will heal.
The angels bring peace,
all conflicts will cease.
With angels of light,
we soar to new height.

**The rustling sound of angel wings,
what joy as even matter sings,
what joy as every atom rings,
in harmony with angel wings.**

## Part 3

1. Serapis Bey, help me see that if my focus is on avoiding making a mistake, then I am not actually being creative. Creativity is not me relating to the material world and current conditions. Creativity is me relating to my I AM Presence and allowing my individuality and creativity to be expressed in the material world.

## 17 | Invoking Freedom to Create

Serapis Bey, what power lies,
behind your purifying eyes.
Serapis Bey, it is a treat,
to enter your sublime retreat.

**O Holy Spirit, flow through me,
I am the open door for thee.
O mighty rushing stream of Light,
transcendence is my sacred right.**

2. Serapis Bey, help me see that creativity is not a matter of trying to avoid negative consequences. It is a matter of being creative so that I either transcend or change the conditions that are creating negative consequences.

Serapis Bey, what wisdom found,
your words are always most profound.
Serapis Bey, I tell you true,
my mind has room for naught but you.

**O Holy Spirit, flow through me,
I am the open door for thee.
O mighty rushing stream of Light,
transcendence is my sacred right.**

3. Serapis Bey, help me become a genius in my everyday life by being creative and learning how to use my built-in, Divine, spiritual creativity to create the life and the life experience I desire in this lifetime so that it can facilitate my growth.

Serapis Bey, what love beyond,
my heart does leap, as I respond.
Serapis Bey, your life a poem,
that calls me to my starry home.

**O Holy Spirit, flow through me,
I am the open door for thee.
O mighty rushing stream of Light,
transcendence is my sacred right.**

4. Serapis Bey, help me see that fulfilling my Divine plan for this lifetime may require that I do some things that from the perspective of other people in my environment can seem irrational, irresponsible or strange.

Serapis Bey, your guidance sure,
my base is clear and white and pure.
Serapis Bey, no longer trapped,
by soul in which my self was wrapped.

**O Holy Spirit, flow through me,
I am the open door for thee.
O mighty rushing stream of Light,
transcendence is my sacred right.**

5. Serapis Bey, help me see that if I make an intuitive connection with my I AM Presence and then go into the analytical mind, I have shut off the creative flow. My I AM Presence must step back, respect my free will and not express itself through me.

> Serapis Bey, what healing balm,
> in mind that is forever calm.
> Serapis Bey, my thoughts are pure,
> your discipline I shall endure.

> **O Holy Spirit, flow through me,**
> **I am the open door for thee.**
> **O mighty rushing stream of Light,**
> **transcendence is my sacred right.**

6. Serapis Bey, help me see that the only way to know what the Presence is going to do through me is to experience it as it is happening. I cannot know ahead of time. I need to let the Presence express what it wants to express.

> Serapis Bey, what secret test,
> for egos who want to be best.
> Serapis Bey, expose in me,
> all that is less than harmony.

> **O Holy Spirit, flow through me,**
> **I am the open door for thee.**
> **O mighty rushing stream of Light,**
> **transcendence is my sacred right.**

7. Serapis Bey, help me see the law that I cannot be connected to my Presence and at the same time be evaluating what the Presence should express. I cannot connect to my Presence through the analytical mind.

Serapis Bey, what moving sight,
my self ascends to sacred height.
Serapis Bey, forever free,
in sacred synchronicity.

**O Holy Spirit, flow through me,
I am the open door for thee.
O mighty rushing stream of Light,
transcendence is my sacred right.**

8. Serapis Bey, help me overcome the fear of my own creativity and the belief that the only way to avoid bad consequences is to control everything. Help me overcome my fear of being spontaneous; my fear of what is unpredictable.

Serapis Bey, you balance all,
the seven rays upon my call.
Serapis Bey, in space and time,
the pyramid of self, I climb.

**O Holy Spirit, flow through me,
I am the open door for thee.
O mighty rushing stream of Light,
transcendence is my sacred right.**

9. Serapis Bey, help me see that the Christ consciousness is when I am connected to my I AM Presence and the I AM Presence can express itself through me. I can of my own self do nothing; it is the I AM Presence within me who is doing the work.

## 17 | Invoking Freedom to Create

> Serapis Bey, your Presence here,
> filling up my inner sphere.
> Life is now a sacred flow,
> God Purity I do bestow.
>
> **O Holy Spirit, flow through me,
> I am the open door for thee.
> O mighty rushing stream of Light,
> transcendence is my sacred right.**

## Part 4

1. Serapis Bey, help me bring what I learn at your retreat down through the identity, mental, emotional body and finally into the physical.

> Saint Germain, your alchemy,
> with violet fire now sets me free.
> Saint Germain, I ever grow,
> in freedom's overpowering flow.
>
> **O Holy Spirit, flow through me,
> I am the open door for thee.
> O mighty rushing stream of Light,
> transcendence is my sacred right.**

2. Serapis Bey, help me see when what is coming to me is from my subconscious mind. Help me see the things in my subconscious mind that are blocking me from attuning to my I AM Presence.

Saint Germain, your mastery,
of violet flame geometry.
Saint Germain, in you I see,
the formulas that set me free.

**O Holy Spirit, flow through me,
I am the open door for thee.
O mighty rushing stream of Light,
transcendence is my sacred right.**

3. Serapis Bey, help me have the courage to follow my inner directions and make the changes to my outer situation that will advance my spiritual growth and my Divine plan.

Saint Germain, in Liberty,
I feel the love you have for me.
Saint Germain, I do adore,
the violet flame that makes all more.

**O Holy Spirit, flow through me,
I am the open door for thee.
O mighty rushing stream of Light,
transcendence is my sacred right.**

4. Serapis Bey, help me develop the discernment to see when something coming to me from within is not from my I AM Presence or the ascended masters, but is from a certain aspect of my ego.

Saint Germain, in unity,
I will transcend duality.
Saint Germain, my self so pure,
your violet chemistry so sure.

> O Holy Spirit, flow through me,
> I am the open door for thee.
> O mighty rushing stream of Light,
> transcendence is my sacred right.

5. Serapis Bey, help me come to the point where I consciously see that this is not a higher direction, this is not something coming from a higher source. Help me consciously recognize this, expose an aspect of my ego and then increase my attunement with my I AM Presence and get real directions from Above.

> Saint Germain, reality,
> in violet light I am carefree.
> Saint Germain, my aura seal,
> your violet flame my chakras heal.

> O Holy Spirit, flow through me,
> I am the open door for thee.
> O mighty rushing stream of Light,
> transcendence is my sacred right.

6. Serapis Bey, help me develop the discernment to see when my inner direction comes from beings in the mental or the identity realm or from my identity body or mental body. Help me see when the purpose is to come to the point where I realize that this is not the highest, there is something higher.

> Saint Germain, your chemistry,
> with violet fire set atoms free.
> Saint Germain, from lead to gold,
> transforming vision I behold.

> O Holy Spirit, flow through me,
> I am the open door for thee.
> O mighty rushing stream of Light,
> transcendence is my sacred right.

7. Serapis Bey, help me see that sometimes the path seems complicated because when I am looking from inside my own mind, it is difficult to see the mechanisms I have created. I created these mechanisms to give myself the illusion that I am a separate being.

> Saint Germain, transcendency,
> as I am always one with thee.
> Saint Germain, from soul I'm free,
> I so delight in being me.

> **O Holy Spirit, flow through me,**
> **I am the open door for thee.**
> **O mighty rushing stream of Light,**
> **transcendence is my sacred right.**

8. Serapis Bey, help me see that I am not a separate being, that it is all an illusion. Help me know that by taking one step at a time, I am thinning the veil and there will come points when the clouds will part and I see a ray of the sun of my I AM Presence.

> Saint Germain, nobility,
> the key to sacred alchemy.
> Saint Germain, you balance all,
> the seven rays upon my call.

> O Holy Spirit, flow through me,
> I am the open door for thee.
> O mighty rushing stream of Light,
> transcendence is my sacred right.

9. Serapis Bey, help me consciously tune in to the Presence that you are. I want to experience your Presence with my outer mind so it can anchor the growth I have gone through at the etheric level in my physical life and outer mind.

> Saint Germain, your Presence here,
> filling up my inner sphere.
> Life is now a sacred flow,
> God Freedom I on all bestow.

> O Holy Spirit, flow through me,
> I am the open door for thee.
> O mighty rushing stream of Light,
> transcendence is my sacred right.

## *Sealing:*

In the name of the Divine Mother, I fully accept that the power of these calls is used to set free the Ma-ter light, so it can outpicture the perfect vision of Christ for my own life, for all people and for the planet. In the name I AM THAT I AM, it is done! Amen.

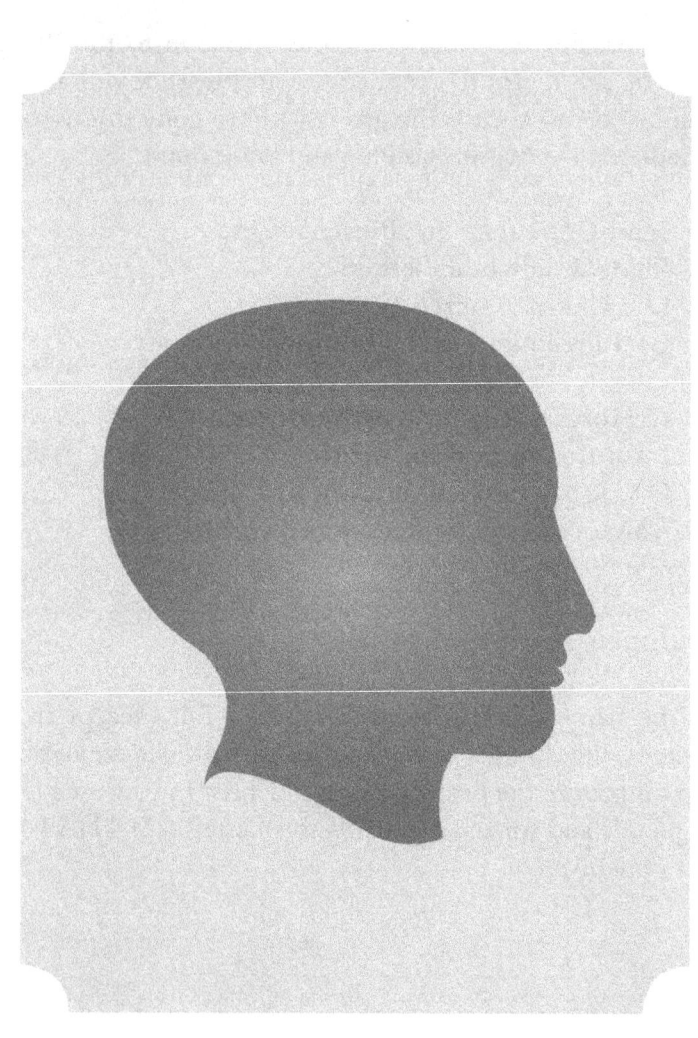

# 4.01 DECREE TO ASTREA AND PURITY

In the name I AM THAT I AM, Jesus Christ, I call to my I AM Presence to flow through the I Will Be Presence that I AM and give these decrees with full power. I call to beloved Elohim Purity and Astrea to help me accelerate my intentions. Help me be accelerate myself beyond all patterns that separate me from my I AM Presence, including …

[Make personal calls]

1. Beloved Astrea, your heart is so true,
your Circle and Sword of white and blue,
cut all life free from dramas unwise,
on wings of Purity our planet will rise.

**Beloved Astrea, in God Purity,
accelerate all of my life energy,
raising my mind into true unity
with the Masters of love in Infinity.**

2. Beloved Astrea, from Purity's Ray,
send forth deliverance to all life today,
acceleration to Purity, I AM now free
from all that is less than love's Purity.

**Beloved Astrea, in oneness with you,**
**your circle and sword of electric blue,**
**with Purity's Light cutting right through,**
**raising within me all that is true.**

3. Beloved Astrea, accelerate us all,
as for your deliverance I fervently call,
set all life free from vision impure
beyond fear and doubt, I AM rising for sure.

**Beloved Astrea, I AM willing to see,**
**all of the lies that keep me unfree,**
**I AM rising beyond every impurity,**
**with Purity's Light forever in me.**

4. Beloved Astrea, accelerate life
beyond all duality's struggle and strife,
consume all division between God and man,
accelerate fulfillment of God's perfect plan.

**Beloved Astrea, I lovingly call,**
**break down separation's invisible wall,**
**I surrender all lies causing the fall,**
**forever affirming the oneness of All.**

Accelerate into Purity, I AM real,
Accelerate into Purity, all life heal,
Accelerate into Purity, I AM MORE,
Accelerate into Purity, all will soar.

Accelerate into Purity! (3X)
Beloved Elohim Astrea.
Accelerate into Purity! (3X)
Beloved Gabriel and Hope.
Accelerate into Purity! (3X)
Beloved Serapis Bey.
Accelerate into Purity! (3X)
Beloved I AM.

## Sealing:

In the name of the Divine Mother, I fully accept that the power of these calls is used to set free the Ma-ter light, so it can outpicture the perfect vision of Christ for my own life, for all people and for the planet. In the name I AM THAT I AM, it is done! Amen.

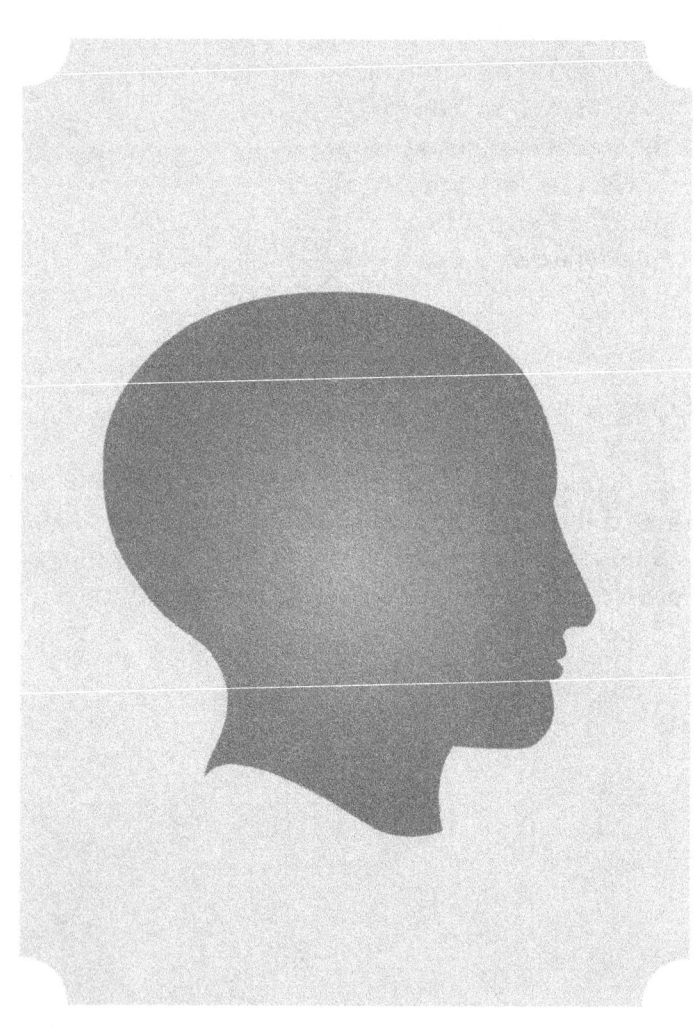

# 4.02 DECREE TO GABRIEL AND HOPE

In the name I AM THAT I AM, Jesus Christ, I call to my I AM Presence to flow through the I Will Be Presence that I AM and give these decrees with full power. I call to beloved Archangel Gabriel and Hope to help me accelerate my intentions. Help me be accelerate myself beyond all patterns that separate me from my I AM Presence, including …

[Make personal calls]

1. Gabriel Archangel, your light I revere,
immersed in your Presence, nothing I fear.
A disciple of Christ, I do leave behind,
the ego's desire for responding in kind.

**Gabriel Archangel, of this I am sure,
Gabriel Archangel, Christ light is the cure.
Gabriel Archangel, intentions so pure,
Gabriel Archangel, in you I'm secure.**

2. Gabriel Archangel, I fear not the light,
in purifications' fire, I delight.
With your hand in mine, each challenge I face,
I follow the spiral to infinite grace.

**Gabriel Archangel, of this I am sure,**
**Gabriel Archangel, Christ light is the cure.**
**Gabriel Archangel, intentions so pure,**
**Gabriel Archangel, in you I'm secure.**

3. Gabriel Archangel, your fire burning white,
ascending with you, out of the night.
My ego has nowhere to run and to hide,
in ascension's bright spiral, with you I abide.

**Gabriel Archangel, of this I am sure,**
**Gabriel Archangel, Christ light is the cure.**
**Gabriel Archangel, intentions so pure,**
**Gabriel Archangel, in you I'm secure.**

4. Gabriel Archangel, your trumpet I hear,
announcing the birth of Christ drawing near.
In lightness of being, I now am reborn,
rising with Christ on bright Easter morn.

**Gabriel Archangel, of this I am sure,**
**Gabriel Archangel, Christ light is the cure.**
**Gabriel Archangel, intentions so pure,**
**Gabriel Archangel, in you I'm secure.**

With angels I soar,
as I reach for MORE.
The angels so real,
their love all will heal.
The angels bring peace,
all conflicts will cease.
With angels of light,
we soar to new height.

**The rustling sound of angel wings,**
**what joy as even matter sings,**
**what joy as every atom rings,**
**in harmony with angel wings.**

## *Sealing:*

In the name of the Divine Mother, I fully accept that the power of these calls is used to set free the Ma-ter light, so it can outpicture the perfect vision of Christ for my own life, for all people and for the planet. In the name I AM THAT I AM, it is done! Amen.

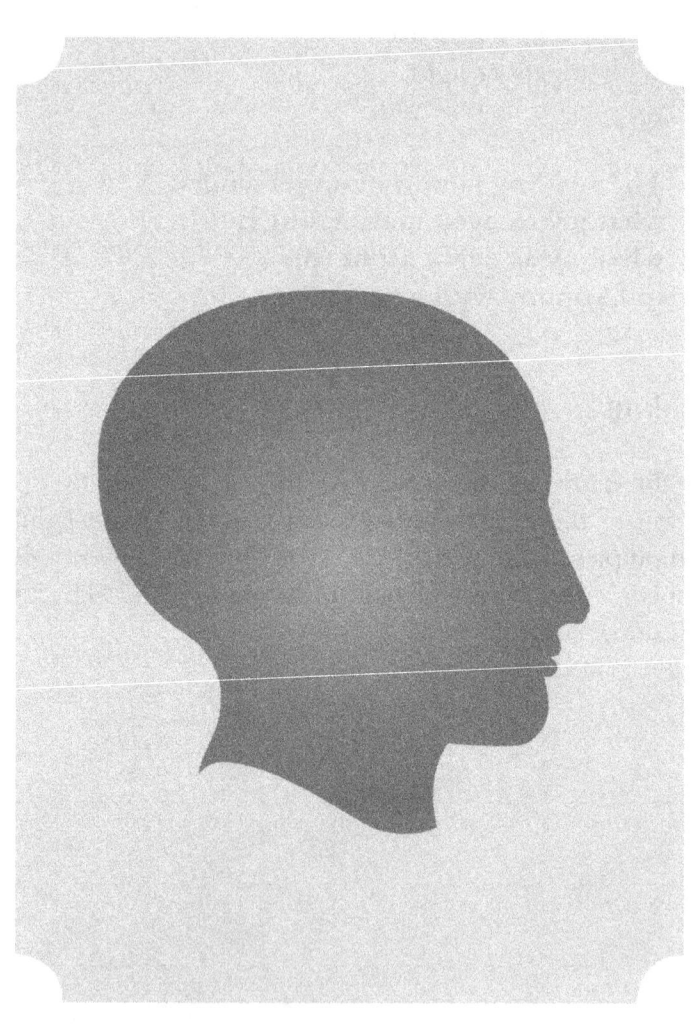

## 4.03 DECREE TO SERAPIS BEY

In the name I AM THAT I AM, Jesus Christ, I call to my I AM Presence to flow through the I Will Be Presence that I AM and give these decrees with full power. I call to beloved Serapis Bey to help me accelerate my intentions. Help me be accelerate myself beyond all patterns that separate me from my I AM Presence, including …

[Make personal calls]

1. Serapis Bey, what power lies,
behind your purifying eyes.
Serapis Bey, it is a treat,
to enter your sublime retreat.

**O Holy Spirit, flow through me,
I am the open door for thee.
O mighty rushing stream of Light,
transcendence is my sacred right.**

2. Serapis Bey, what wisdom found,
your words are always most profound.
Serapis Bey, I tell you true,
my mind has room for naught but you.

**O Holy Spirit, flow through me,
I am the open door for thee.
O mighty rushing stream of Light,
transcendence is my sacred right.**

3. Serapis Bey, what love beyond,
my heart does leap, as I respond.
Serapis Bey, your life a poem,
that calls me to my starry home.

**O Holy Spirit, flow through me,
I am the open door for thee.
O mighty rushing stream of Light,
transcendence is my sacred right.**

4. Serapis Bey, your guidance sure,
my base is clear and white and pure.
Serapis Bey, no longer trapped,
by soul in which my self was wrapped.

**O Holy Spirit, flow through me,
I am the open door for thee.
O mighty rushing stream of Light,
transcendence is my sacred right.**

5. Serapis Bey, what healing balm,
in mind that is forever calm.
Serapis Bey, my thoughts are pure,
your discipline I shall endure.

**O Holy Spirit, flow through me,
I am the open door for thee.
O mighty rushing stream of Light,
transcendence is my sacred right.**

6. Serapis Bey, what secret test,
for egos who want to be best.
Serapis Bey, expose in me,
all that is less than harmony.

**O Holy Spirit, flow through me,
I am the open door for thee.
O mighty rushing stream of Light,
transcendence is my sacred right.**

7. Serapis Bey, what moving sight,
my self ascends to sacred height.
Serapis Bey, forever free,
in sacred synchronicity.

**O Holy Spirit, flow through me,
I am the open door for thee.
O mighty rushing stream of Light,
transcendence is my sacred right.**

8. Serapis Bey, you balance all,
the seven rays upon my call.
Serapis Bey, in space and time,
the pyramid of self, I climb.

**O Holy Spirit, flow through me,
I am the open door for thee.
O mighty rushing stream of Light,
transcendence is my sacred right.**

9. Serapis Bey, your Presence here,
filling up my inner sphere.
Life is now a sacred flow,
God Purity I do bestow.

**O Holy Spirit, flow through me,
I am the open door for thee.
O mighty rushing stream of Light,
transcendence is my sacred right.**

## *Sealing:*

In the name of the Divine Mother, I fully accept that the power of these calls is used to set free the Ma-ter light, so it can outpicture the perfect vision of Christ for my own life, for all people and for the planet. In the name I AM THAT I AM, it is done! Amen.

www.ingramcontent.com/pod-product-compliance
Lightning Source LLC
Chambersburg PA
CBHW031421150426
43191CB00006B/350